New Paths through the Old Testament

Carroll Stuhlmueller, C.P.

120147

PAULIST PRESS
New York/Mahwah, N.J.

Imprimi Potest:
Reverend Sebastian MacDonald, C.P.
Provincial
May 9, 1989

Nihil Obstat:
Reverend John G. Lodge, S.S.L.
Censor Deputatus

Imprimatur:
Reverend James P. Roache
Vicar General
Archdiocese of Chicago
May 1, 1989

The *Nihil Obstat* and *Imprimatur* are official declarations that a book or pamphlet is free of doctrinal or moral error. No implication is contained therein that those who have granted the *Nihil Obstat* and *Imprimatur* agree with the content, opinions, or statements expressed.

Library of Congress Cataloging-in-Publication Data

Stuhlmueller, Carroll.
    New paths through the Old Testament/by Carroll Stuhlmueller.
      p. cm.
    Bibliography: p.
    ISBN-0-8091-3094-7: $6.95 (est.)
    1. Bible. O.T.—Criticism, interpretation, etc. I. Title.
BS1171.2.S795   1989
221.6'1—dc20   89-16001
                                         CIP

Published by Paulist Press
997 Macarthur Boulevard
Mahwah, N.J. 07430

Printed and bound in the United States of America

Table of Contents

Foreword

Giving a popular presentation of scholarly insights is always a risky business. In the sphere of Old Testament studies many insights have been gained into everything from the role of shrines in the preservation of traditions to the stamp of a prophet on the keepers and revisers of his work. This book takes the risk and succeeds. It popularizes insights which have proven most useful in Old Testament studies in the last hundred years.

Making complex things simple, difficult things clear and shocking things acceptable is an art which Fr. Stuhlmueller has refined over the years. It is put to very good use in this book. The most important insight he shares is a new understanding of the humanity of the Word. The more we come to understand its earthiness, the more amazingly do we discover that it is truly the word of GOD.

We are all familiar with the image of the sacred writer, alone with the thoughts of God, inspired by a shaft of light coming from heaven. Fr. Carroll enlarges that spotlight into a floodlight, revealing on stage a host of other characters which until recently have been in the shadows. It is good to meet them and to begin to know them.

The book is "user friendly," though it does challenge the reader to take care and to listen attentively to the guide who leads us by the hand. You will enjoy this walk through time and come to appreciate even more the wonder of the Word which is God's.

Marcel Gervais
Bishop of Sault Ste. Marie, Canada
Author of *Journey* (40 lessons on the Bible)

v

Introduction

You are invited as friends of the Bible to approach the Old Testament anew. This book draws upon recent biblical scholarship to chart new paths. At the same time we presume no special knowledge of this scholarship, nor even of the Old Testament.

As a matter of fact, some of the latest scholarship makes itself unnecessary, at least at first, for it is stressing what it calls the "canonical shape" of the Bible. In simple terms "canon" means approaching the Bible *as it is,* from Genesis the first book to Revelation the final book. Israel received the Old Testament and Christianity both Testaments *this way,* as a rule for faith, moral integrity and worship.

We begin in chapters one and two of this book with the Old Testament *as it is.* Nothing more is required than a Bible at hand and the willingness to be a friendly person of faith in opening it. As a friend, we do not argue and belittle, even if we do not understand or if it sounds silly at first. A friend respects a friend. And as a person of faith, we listen reverently to the Bible, realizing that the friend who ultimately takes responsibility for its words is none other than God. Finally, as a friend, we also esteem the human authors who, like the one responsible for the second book of Maccabees, admitted:

> For us who have undertaken the toil of abbreviating [the five volumes of Jason into one], it is no light matter but calls for sweat and loss of sleep, just as it is not easy for one who prepares a banquet and seeks the benefit of others (2 Mac 2:26–27).

1

The authors responsible for individual books and the editors who arranged the books in the sequence of our Old Testament not only worked diligently with "sweat and loss of sleep," but they also acted as reasonable people with a plan and purpose.

The first three chapters of this book search for that plan and purpose. We are working only with the Old Testament. In fact, other books, no matter how scholarly and important, would only intrude right now. We want to approach the Old Testament "hands on." We want to imitate good nurses or physicians who do not turn to X-rays or other mechanical devices, nor administer medicine, until they have carefully examined the human body of the patient and have become acquainted with the family background and life style.

Chapter one looks at the Bible's table of contents and compares the Christian with the Jewish division of the Old Testament —and asks "Why?" Why are the two divisions different? What is unique about each arrangement? And a further question always arises with the Old Testament: Why are there seven more books in Catholic editions of the Bible? And still more books among the Orthodox churches? It is surprising how much mileage we gain simply from examining the table of contents!

Chapter two looks at two books in particular, Exodus and Isaiah, with similar questions: What is unique about the arrangement of chapters? Like a friend walking through the home of a friend, the reader wants to know why this picture is hanging in the living room, why this piece of antique furniture is in the dining room, why this set of dishes is in the kitchen. All have a story and the housekeeper delights in telling it. The flow of chapters in any book of the Bible also has a story and a theological message. So, we look at what is there "hands-on" and ask: Why is it this way? Why does this chapter follow that chapter? The questions are as simple as the air we breathe, as matter-of-fact as our home, and as precious as family heirlooms and their stories. We find the answers best if we first ask them as a friend, with no intrusion from outside. Later, if necessary, we bring in the experts!

Chapter three brings us on a journey from the home to our place of family prayer and worship—in Christian language to our church, in Old Testament language to the sanctuaries and the Jerusalem temple. Again by walking slowly and meditatively through the chapters and books of the Old Testament, as we would through a large church or cathedral, we begin to recognize the importance of religious assemblies to the formation and preservation of the Bible. In fact, most of the Old Testament centers around sacred places. The writers or speakers, especially prophets, may not be always pleased with what they see going on there, but they are always in accord with the centrality of temple and sanctuaries in Israelite life. Otherwise why did they bother so much about them!

Part of our study touches upon the question which comes up almost at once among Christians yet was seldom asked in biblical times: Did it really happen? When? Where? We squarely face the question of history in the Old Testament and conclude that while the Bible rests upon reality, its authors never intended to write history. Theirs is a document for prayer and instruction, frequently updated because of new problems, questions and hopes. Detailed history of individual eras gets lost in the layering of many periods of time in a single text or tradition. Because the Old Testament reflects so much reality over such a long period of time, and because the purpose was always to motivate faithful discipleship (not to prepare archival material), the history of Israel is difficult to reconstruct with definitive certitude.

Before summarizing the history of Old Testament times so that we are better prepared to return to our Bible and place its books and events in a time sequence (this is the task of chapter five of the book), we take our first move into scholarly positions, in this case the four traditions which were eventually combined to produce the Torah or five books of Moses, Genesis through Deuteronomy. Again we recognize the importance of faith as handed down in a family. We are back again, moving through a home and seeing the photos and period pieces of the grandparents. Homes and families are what they are, because the traditions of ancestors have been woven carefully together into the flesh and blood of their descendants, into the personality of the children as well as into the latter's new families. In the traditions behind the five books of Moses we discover what makes Israel different from all other nations and what leads this people determinedly into their future.

Finally in the sixth chapter we ask what is usually a major question among Christians: How does the Old Testament predict the messiah and announce Jesus as redeemer and savior of the world? But questions like this ought to be asked last. When we meet friends and visit their home, we first speak about the present moment, their family and friends, their neighbors and employment. Next we are introduced to the grandparents and a wider circle of relatives. Last of all we dare to venture into plans and expectations for the future of themselves and their children.

The present and the past are real; the future is not yet. What is real we do not fear nearly as much as what is unreal and lies ahead of us. Only from trusted friends do we seek advice about our hopes and our fears. Out of respect for our friend the Old Testament we should first listen to what it meant in its own moment of life, and how it drew this life from its ancestors in the faith. Only after we have become thoroughly acquainted with this background (actually the first five chapters of this book) do we venture into the Old Testament hopes for the future.

The approach to the Old Testament in this book is as normal as broken-in shoes, the easiest to use with the least amount of pain. Yet all the while it is applying some of the latest tools in biblical scholarship to the study of the Old Testament. As we mentioned at the beginning, we start out with the canonical approach, standardized by such scholars as Brevard S. Childs and James A. Sanders. Thomas W. Mann's *The Book of the Torah* (John Knox Press, 1988) focused the canonical inquiry upon the five books of Moses. The salient importance of the liturgical setting and oral tradition for the Old Testament was recognized long ago by German and Scandinavian scholars like Hermann Gunkel and Sigmund Mowinckel. An exceptionally helpful book about Israel's religious assemblies, unfortunately overlooked in most circles, came from Lucien Deiss, *God's Word and God's People* (Liturgical Press, 1976). The history of the Old Testament has been pursued by such veteran scholars as Roland de Vaux and John Bright, while the sociological currents of life within this history have been elaborated for us by Norman Gottwald, Robert

R. Wilson and James W. Flanagan. The different methods for studying the Old Testament have been summarized well by Daniel Harrington in his volume introducing the series, *Old Testament Message* (Michael Glazier, Inc., 1981). Lawrence Boadt's *Reading the Old Testament* (Paulist Press, 1984) picks up all of these methods and proceeds book by book through the entire Old Testament.

These names are but a sampling, with important ones missing. Their books were mentioned as a next step. Our purpose here is to work for the most part *simply with the Bible,* reading it as men and women of faith. We hope to chart new paths so that we can visit with our friend the Old Testament and quietly appreciate the consolation and challenge of the word of God. Ours, as we said, is a "hands-on" approach with our Bible. After we become well acquainted and at home with our friend, after we have attended our friend's place of worship and heard the stories of the ancestors, then we can go to school and read the work of the scholars. Scholarly volumes should not set the attitude or spirit for Bible reading; rather they are intended to enrich, strengthen, open new vistas and correct mistakes.

Last of all, by initially charting new paths through the Old Testament but not to scholarly books, we make a delicate but significant shift in emphasis. The WORD of God which can be studied and pulled apart by scientific enterprise ought to remain or revert back to the Word of GOD. The capitalized letters indicate the center of attention and the shift from study to prayer, from historical investigation to faithful interaction, from rational processes to contemplative silence—from WORD to the living GOD who speaks the word now. Once this approach of faith is secured, then we turn to other more scientific sources and study the WORD of God.

This method is not canonizing fundamentalism nor a rigidly conservative way of reading the Bible. That it is not must be left to the chapters of this book to explain. Here we add just a passing observation: unless contemplation of GOD remains in contact with the living presence of God in human life with its suffering and sin, contemplation runs the serious risk of becoming ecstatic deism or poetic trance. There needs to be a continuous swiveling between the word of GOD . . . and . . . the WORD of God . . . and back again to the word of GOD.

The Bible translations in this book are from the Revised Standard Version. For the few times when this is not the case, my initials (CS) have been added to the citation.

Finally, a word of thanks to friends who helped this book become a reality. The way has been mysterious and, I trust, under God's inspiration, baffling human explanation at times. Without explaining why, for they know, I thank Dr. Robert Delaney of Franciscan Communications in Los Angeles, Rev. Lawrence Boadt of Paulist Press and Sister Marylyn Welter, School Sister of Saint Francis.

The preface of Bishop Marcel Gervais evokes happy memories, especially of the years when he directed the Divine Word International Centre of Religious Education, London, Ontario, and invited me to be a guest lecturer. During those years he composed *Journey,* a guided study program of the Old and New Testaments, available in the USA from Paulist Press.

Earlier in this introduction we quoted from the second book of Maccabees. It is time to turn again to this book and make our own its confession of wordiness:

> It is the duty of the original historian to occupy the ground and to discuss matters from every side and to take trouble with details, but the one who recasts the narrative should be allowed to strive for brevity of expression and to forego exhaustive treatment. At this point therefore let us begin . . . for it is foolish to lengthen the preface while cutting short the history itself (2 Mac 2:28–32).

Chapter One

The Old Testament: A Book of Many Books

Some years ago while teaching a college course on the Old Testament, a student asked me: "Why do you call a chapter a book and why do you say that sections of a chapter are actually chapters all by themselves?" At first I thought that he was trapping me in a question of biblical trivia. Yet he was not only serious but dead right—and somewhat uninformed about the Bible!

A Different Kind of Book

First of all, the student was right in questioning why we call parts of the Bible, for instance, Genesis or Isaiah, a book, when they are parts of a single book under one binding. We ought to designate Genesis and Isaiah chapters in this single book called the Bible.

The Bible, however, is not a regular kind of book. The very word *Bible* derives from the Greek, *biblia* (neuter, plural), signifying "books." This fact flashes a signal that the Bible is a collection of many books, of different sizes, styles and content. Though inspired by one Holy Spirit, its sections were not written at a single sitting by one human author. It needs to be studied across a thousand or more years of history.

The Bible is more complicated than that, especially when we remember, as Pope Pius XII wrote in a famous letter on the Bible, that the many human authors contributed their own outlook, vocabulary and literary form. We can infer, the pope stated, "the special character of each one and, as it were, their personal traits." The individual authors of each book, therefore, need to be taken seriously. Otherwise, again quoting from Pope Pius XII, "we miss the real meaning."

How Is It an "Old" Testament?

Another problem arises with the expression "Old Testament." It is the normal way for Christians to refer to the first and largest section of their Bible. Yet for Jesus it was by no means an "old" testament; it was Jesus' only Bible, a living word of God, ever new, awaiting fulfillment in his person and mission, as it is still awaiting fulfillment in our lives, our church, our world. As Jesus declared on Easter Sunday night to the apostles: "Everything written about me in the law of Moses and the prophets and the psalms must be fulfilled" (Lk 24:44). The New Testament refers to the Old Testament as "the law and the prophets" (Mt 5:17), or to a passage of it as "spoken by the prophet Joel" (Acts 2:16). The term "Old Testament" was not used till the late second century A.D. and is based upon such passages as 2 Corinthians 3:14 and Hebrews 8:7. For instance:

> For if that first covenant had been faultless, there would have been no occasion for a second. . . . In speaking of a new covenant he treats the first as obsolete. And what is becoming obsolete and growing old is ready to vanish away (Heb 8:7, 13).

Yet the epistle to the Hebrews is not confining the earlier scriptures to a museum. Otherwise, why would it have quoted from them to understand the mission of Jesus? Hebrews, instead, is declaring that older interpretations must give way to new insights through the birth, death and resurrection of Jesus.

The New Testament is continually interweaving words and sentences of the Old Testament into its own exposition of the mystery of Jesus. Jesus in turn casts new light upon the mystery hidden within the Old Testament. "Old" means earlier and basic, not antiquated and displaced. Paul wrote to his disciple Timothy:

CLASS NO. 304-7	AUTHOR Stuhlmueller, Carr		
ACCESSION NO.	TITLE New Paths through the O.T.		
COPIES ORDERED			
DATE ORDERED	PLACE AND PUBLISHER Paulist	YEAR	
	EDITION OR SERIES Paulist	1989	
FROM Paulist		LIST 1.00	
DATE RECEIVED	ILLUSTRATOR	NO. OF COPIES 1.00	
COST 1.00	DEPT. FOR WHICH RECOMMENDED	REVIEWED	
L.C. OR WILSON CARD	TEACHER S. Kilbern		
HIGHSMITH 46-183			

And how from childhood you have been acquainted with the sacred writings [the books of our Old Testament] which are able to instruct you for salvation through faith in Christ Jesus. *All* scripture is inspired by God and profitable for teaching, for reproof, for correction, and for training in righteousness, that the godly person may be complete, equipped for every good work (2 Tim 3:15–16).

Paul refers to the religious instruction which he received "from childhood." We are reminded of another statement which tells of his attachment to Timothy's family and the warm sensitivity of Paul's character:

As I remember your tears, I long night and day to see you, that I may be filled with joy. I am reminded of your sincere faith, a faith that dwelt first in your grandmother Lois and your mother Eunice and now I am sure, dwells in you (2 Tim 1:4–5).

Bible study begins at home at an early age.

The Old Testament, as already noted, consists of many books from many authors over many centuries, addressing many problems and hopes. These books were edited and gathered together according to two different plans, one Christian and another Jewish. This latter one is earlier and was prevalent in the time of Jesus; the former evolved over several centuries, first in Egypt among Jewish people and later among Christians. We have much to learn from each.

The Christian Table of Contents

We look first at the table of contents in the *New Jerusalem Bible* (1985) with some comparison with that in the *New American Bible* (1970; 1986). The books of the Old Testament are subdivided into (a) the Pentateuch and Historical Books, (b) the Wisdom Books, and (c) the Prophetical Books.

(a) *Pentateuch:* Genesis, Exodus, Leviticus, Numbers, Deuteronomy

   Historical Books:

Joshua	1–2 Samuel	Ezra	Judith
Judges	1–2 Kings	Nehemiah	Esther
Ruth	1–2 Chronicles	Tobit	1–2 Maccabees

(b) *Wisdom Books*

Job	Proverbs	Wisdom
Psalms	Ecclesiastes	Sirach (Ecclesiasticus)
	Song of Songs	

(c) *Prophetical Books*
   4 Major: Isaiah, Jeremiah (+ Lamentations and Baruch), Ezekiel, Daniel
   12 Minor: Hosea, Joel, Amos, Obadiah, Jonah, Micah, Nahum, Habakkuk, Zephaniah, Haggai, Zechariah, Malachi

What at first seems like a random grocery list in the Bible's table of contents upon further investigation manifests important religious objectives.

Historical books and prophetical books are the two conspicuous sections, not only in the number of books but also in their place at the beginning and the end of the Old Testament. In earlier Christian editions of the Bible, even the Pentateuch was listed under historical books. Each moment of time was thought to be leading forward to the coming of the messiah. That moment will be "the fullness of time" when God has "made known to us in all wisdom and insight the mystery of God's will, according to a purpose set forth in Christ" (Eph 1:9–10). The historical books move from the first moment of creation in the opening lines of Genesis, to the account of the final great persecution before the coming of the messiah in first and second Maccabees.

As a result, Christians have stressed the *historical* aspects of the Bible. While this approach is not incorrect, still during the last two centuries it has sometimes been done so emphatically and even so belligerently that the Bible was considered almost nothing other than a history book. Its trustworthiness, many people felt, stood or fell on the dependability of each statement to describe exactly what happened, even in the smallest details. Accuracy was determined from what was obvious to an eye witness or to a twentieth century reader.

History as reflected in biblical books must be judged according to two important criteria. First, how did *ancient* people speak of events? Second, what *religious instruction* is the Bible imparting when it speaks about events? Ancient historians wrote in one of two ways: (a) *a list of statistics,* for instance, what cities were conquered, by whom, and when, as we see upon the temple walls at Karnak in Egypt or in Joshua 12 and 2 Samuel 8; (b) *stories* to exalt the heavenly gods and the earthly kings, again as found upon the temple walls of Karnak or in Joshua 1–8.

Statistics and stories each provide a valid insight into what is happening. Statistics are objectively more accurate but dry and impersonal; stories are subjectively more intent upon imparting the faith and the feeling, the intricate human factors, the personal investment of hopes and pain. Biblical stories involve the listeners intensely in the ancient event. Stories communicate less about the surface, much more about the depth of meaning. For this reason Jesus taught more by stories and parables than by doctrinal statements.

We must be careful not to fall into the trap of thinking that ancient people had to write history as we do. Nor should we be led down another false way of thinking that stories have no objective truth. Stories pick up many details from ancient times but put the facts into the form of conversations, prayers, hymns, visions and dreams. These literary forms give us insights into what is otherwise inexpressible. Neither should we overlook the religious purpose of biblical stories, based upon real events but intending most of all to teach and inspire later generations about God's presence in *their* lives.

Still another trap is the tendency to restrict prophecy, the other important section in our table of contents, to prediction of details like the place or the time of the messiah's birth or death. Prophecy involved much more than predicting the future.

Prophets were social reformers in the name of a compassionate
God, as we read in Micah 2–3; they were mystics and teachers
of prayer, in close touch with God, as in Ezekiel 1–3 or in
Zechariah 1. Prophets struggled through darkness and were un-
certain about themselves and their message. Certainly that was
the case with Jeremiah (12:1–5; 20:7–18). Messianic prediction,
moreover, included more than details. It was carried forward by
disciples who were poor and persecuted (Jer 37–38; Is 49:1–7;
50:3–9), so that Jesus fulfilled prophecy by identifying himself as
much with an oppressed and neglected people as with their
words (Mt 8:1–17).

New books were being added to the Old Testament right up
to the time of Jesus. In the table of contents we notice the way
that Lamentations and Baruch (the latter was especially late in its
composition) were attached to the prophecy of Jeremiah. In
Egypt the book of Wisdom was considered inspired, though written as late as fifty or twenty years before the birth of Jesus. In
Palestine the devout Jews who lived along the Dead Sea and were
responsible for copying the Dead Sea Scrolls venerated the book
of Sirach. Two manuscripts of it were discovered, one at Qumran
and the other at nearby Masada.

It is important, therefore, to become acquainted with the
Bible as it is. It may not be all that strange to study the table of
contents!

The Jewish Table of Contents

Because the Old Testament came to us from the Jewish people, their ancient way of dividing the books will also be helpful.
We notice significant divergence from the Christian arrangement.
Because this disposition of books was current in the days of Jesus,
we need to attend to it.

Jews call their Bible either "The Holy Scriptures" or
"Tanak." The first title is self-explanatory, but not the second.
The consonants in Tanak come from the first letters of three
Hebrew words: Torah (or law and instruction), Neviim (or
prophets), and Kethubim (or writings). These three words are the
titles for the three major parts of the Hebrew Bible.

While the word "Tanak" was not used in the Old and New Testaments, nonetheless its way of dividing the holy scriptures was current. When the book of Sirach was being translated, the author's grandson wrote affectionately in his preface about "my grandfather Jesus [the full name, as we saw in the Introduction of this book, was Jesus the son of Eleazar, the son of Sirach, Sir 50:27] . . . devoting himself especially to the reading of the law and the prophets and the other books of our ancestors." Another, much better known person with the name of Jesus referred to the Bible either as "the law and the prophets" (Mt 5:17) or "the law of Moses and the prophets and the psalms" (Lk 24:44). "Psalms" here refer to the Kethubim or Writings, as it is the first book in this section.

The Jewish holy scriptures divide accordingly:

(a) Torah or Five Books of Moses: Genesis, Exodus, Leviticus, Numbers and Deuteronomy;

(b) Neviim or Prophets
    Former Prophets: Joshua, Judges, 1–2 Samuel, 1–2 Kings
    Latter Prophets:
        3 major: Isaiah, Jeremiah, Ezekiel
        12 minor: as listed above

(c) Kethubim or Writings
    Psalms, Proverbs, Job
    Megilloth or "Scrolls" for special feasts
        Song of Songs, for the feast of Passover
        Ruth, for the feast of Weeks or Pentecost
        Lamentations for the feast mourning the destruction of the temple
        Ecclesiastes, for the feast of Tabernacles
        Esther, for the feast of Purim
    Daniel, Ezra and Nehemiah, 1–2 Chronicles

In the Jewish division we recognize no special division called "historical books." Jewish people have the greatest respect for tradition and history. Nonetheless, they do not look upon their Bible as *primarily* a history book. Rather it is considered most of all a book of instruction and prayer, whose meaning can never be exhausted.

The five books of Moses, the Torah, are supreme, and, like our gospels, stand separately by themselves. The Torah itself canonizes Moses on several occasions. It states that when Moses came down from Mount Sinai, the skin of his face shone so brilliantly that he had to wear a veil over his face when conversing with the people (Ex 34:29–34). There is the lovely passage in Numbers 12:3, declaring that Moses "was very meek, more than anyone on the face of the earth" (CS). Again, the last words of the Torah declare:

> There has not arisen a prophet since in Israel like Moses, whom the LORD knew face to face, none like him for all the signs and the wonders which the LORD sent him to do in the land of Egypt . . . and for all the mighty power and all the great and fearsome deeds which Moses wrought in the sight of all Israel (Dt 34:10–12, CS).

As unique and authoritative as it is, the Torah had to be brought into touch with the ongoing life of Israel. In the synagogues, therefore, it was never read alone but was always joined with a passage from the prophetical books, either the former or the latter.

Books like Joshua and Judges or 1–2 Samuel and 1–2 Kings were not placed in a category called "historical books" but rather were considered prophecy. Prophecy manifested the various ways by which Israel was judged by the norms and hopes of the Torah or by which Israel adapted the generic principles of the Torah to the more specific circumstances of daily life. While royalty had little importance in the Torah, the prophetical books bowed to the demands of the time and made it one of the pivotal points of life. Prophecy is not the final section of the Bible, as in the Christian Old Testament. Rather it is placed second, to be followed by the Kethubim or "the Writings."

"Writings" show the ever more important place of temple

worship. This section begins with Psalms, more than anything else the temple prayer book. "Writings" include the "Megilloth," the Hebrew word for "scrolls," unrolled and read on the major feasts. Finally, "Writings" conclude with 1–2 Chronicles. In 1 Chronicles 25:1 psalm writers and singers are set apart to "prophesy with lyres, with harps, and with cymbals." Prophecy is no longer the fiery condemnation of social abuses, nor the agonizing vigil, watching the collapse of a nation. Rather prophecy returns to the sanctuary, as we see in 1 Samuel 10:5–8, and manifests itself enthusiastically in worship.

1–2 Chronicles ends, as does the entire holy scriptures of the Jewish people, with the decree of Cyrus, charging the Israelites to build the temple at Jerusalem where all God's people will assemble. The very last words of the Hebrew Bible are: "Let them go up" to the Jerusalem temple. By contrast the Christian arrangement concludes with the prophetical announcement of the coming of the messenger and the Lord to the temple (Mal 3:1), preceded by Elijah the prophet (Mal 4:5–6), texts quoted at the beginning of Mark's gospel (Mk 1:2–8). The Jewish division centered upon the temple, the Christian division upon "something greater than the temple [that] is here" (Mt 12:6), namely, the messianic moment.

A Larger and Smaller Table of Contents

If we compare the table of contents in Catholic editions of the Bible with that of Jewish and Protestant editions, we notice seven more books: Tobit and Judith, 1–2 Maccabees among the historical books; Wisdom and Sirach among the wisdom books; Baruch among the prophetical books. Parts of the books of Esther and Daniel are also not shared by Protestant and Jewish editions. The Greek churches extend the number of books to include 3–4 Maccabees, the prayer of Manasseh, and Psalm 151. In Russia 2 Esdras is venerated as part of the Bible, and in Ethiopia still more books.

We deliberately speak of Jewish, Protestant and Catholic *editions* of the Bible rather than Jewish, Protestant and Catholic

Bibles. Granted these differences, there is basically only *one* Bible for Christians and only *one* Old Testament or Tanak for Christians and Jews.

Catholics call these sections that are not found in Jewish and Protestant editions the "deutero-canonical" books; Protestants use the word "apocrypha." Deutero-canonical means the second or wider canon; apocrypha means concealed or hidden. These books were either unknown or later under dispute by some sectors of Jews and Christians. What is undisputed, however, is the openness of the Bible to new books in the days of Jesus. There was never any challenge or controversy about that fact.

A larger collection than that circulating at Jerusalem existed among the Jewish people in Egypt, responsible for translating the sacred books from Hebrew into Greek, and among those other Jews living at Qumran along the northwest shore of the Dead Sea. The Jews at Qumran were not a radical fringe group. They were so zealous for the law of Moses that at least a quorum of ten took turns reciting the law all through the day and night in obedience to the injunction in Joshua 1:8. Some manuscripts at Qumran arranged the psalms differently than what is now found in our book of Psalms. They also included Psalm 151 as well as other songs or canticles, until now unknown to us. The Dead Sea Scrolls also seem to have recognized as part of their holy scriptures the books of Tobit, Sirach, the letter of Jeremiah, Jubilees and Enoch. The first two of these books are still in Catholic editions of the Bible, the third within the Bible of the Greek churches; the last two, quite popular in the early church, have fallen by the way.

The discussion of what books belong in our Bible becomes still more complicated when we recall that other books, firmly in place in all Bibles today, were under serious dispute among the rabbis in the days of Jesus: books like Ezekiel, Ecclesiastes and the Song of Songs. We read in an ancient rabbinical source, the Babylonian Talmud, that speculations about the meaning of the opening chapters of Ezekiel were so dangerous that of four scholars who tackled such a task, one lost his reason, another died, one turned skeptic, and only one survived uninjured. It also speaks of

Rabbi Hananiah ben Hezekiah who locked himself in a room until he resolved all the discrepancies. Still another rabbi concluded that such passages as Ezekiel 44:31 and 45:18 would be adequately explained only when the prophet Elijah reappeared upon the earth.

With these, as with all rabbinical stories, there is a blend of light humor with deadly seriousness. God must be amused at times over the squabbles among saintly scholars.

Seriously we see that the Bible was open-ended in the time of Jesus and the early church. Crises in the first century after the death of Jesus demanded a clear decision about what books belonged in the Bible. With the destruction of Jerusalem and the scattering of Jewish people throughout the Roman empire, the Jews felt the need of finding stability in the holy scriptures as fixed and determined for everyone. Theological problems and the appearance of heretical groups among Christians who were writing their own sacred books led to some resolution about what books at least did not belong in the Bible. These controversies lasted for several hundred years. Throughout this time Jews favored a more restricted number of books, while Christians adopted a more expanded Bible. The Greek translation of the Jews in Egypt became the standard Bible of Christianity. The major norm in this decision came from pastoral practice: Which books were used for worship and instruction over a long period of time? The Council of Trent used the same norm in declaring the seven deutero-canonical books to be part of the inspired scriptures.

The Jews, therefore, ended up with a shorter "canon," the technical word for what belongs in the Bible as a norm of faith. ("Canon" is a transliteration of a Hebrew word for reed or stalk which grows in swampy areas and when cut and trimmed was used at times as a yardstick or ruler; thence came the transfer to what was a norm or rule of faith and prayer.) In Christianity the controversy was stirred by St. Jerome (A.D. 340?–420), so dedicated to the Hebrew text that he refused to consider anything else. Yet the rest of the church passed him by. The Council of Trullo II (A.D. 692) declared for a larger canon than the Jewish. The issue was never raised until the time of the Protestant reformation when a definitive decree did come from the Catholic Church at the Council of Trent (April 8, 1548).

At the time of the Protestant reformation Luther, Calvin and the other reformers returned to the Hebrew language of the Old Testament instead of relying upon the Latin Vulgate, and in so doing were moved to accept only those books found in the Hebrew editions of the Bible. The reformers relegated the deuterocanonical books ("apocrypha" is their name for them) to an appendix. Eventually the appendix was dropped. It was at this same time that other differences showed up among Jews, Protestants and Catholics, for instance, in the way that the Bible was divided into chapters and verses, or in the enumeration of the psalms.

In Conclusion

Some topics which we discussed in this opening chapter were admittedly difficult and involved, so much so that we simply alerted ourselves to one of them, the separation into chapters and verses, where different versions manifest small but frequent differences.

Other types of problems came to our attention: for instance, the different ways of writing historical accounts in ancient times, somewhat diverse from our modern ways of doing it. These facts flash a signal across the dashboard of our desk that the study of the Bible at times requires close attention and perhaps expert direction.

Much can be learned by applying ourselves to the table of contents and asking ourselves: Why are the books arranged the way they are? Christians want to stress that each moment of time, then as now, leads up to the manifestation of Jesus as Lord and savior. Prophecy is a judgment upon life to point out the need of such a messiah. The Jewish division points out the supreme importance of the Torah or five books of Moses and of the Jerusalem temple to which everyone comes in pilgrimage. Jews also recognize the need of explaining and adapting the Torah to everyday life and its new problems. They meet this demand through a section of their Bible called "prophetical books." They were never drawn into the trap of falsely understanding biblical history as a mirror held up to the external details of life.

Still another way of reviewing this chapter is to chart a method for opening the Bible at prayer or study:

First, scan the table of contents and ask yourself why the books are arranged in this fashion, from Pentateuch and historical books, to wisdom literature, to prophecy. The historical books insist on the importance of God's interaction in human life, here on planet earth. History, however, is not understood so much as a record of events (it is that, but much more) as it presents models for God's presence with us today. Prophecy, for its part, advises us that each moment is leading to an ever fuller manifestation of Jesus, messiah and savior.

Second, see how the Old Testament was continually adding new books, like the additions of Lamentations and Baruch to the tradition centering round the prophet Jeremiah, or the seven books found in Roman Catholic editions of the Bible but not in Jewish and Protestant editions. Here it is helpful to compare Bibles—and ask: "Why the difference?"

Third, realize that the basic Old Testament series of books from Moses, the first five which are called the Torah in Jewish editions of the Bible, cannot stand alone but need prophecy and other writings. Today for Christians the Old Testament cannot be properly interpreted without the New Testament, and both together without church tradition. Tradition parallels the way in which the Torah was applied and adapted throughout the history of the people Israel.

When the Old Testament becomes, as Vatican II desired, "the strength of faith, the food of the soul, the pure and perennial source of spiritual life," when its spiritual value is recognized and absorbed for consolation and instruction, as Paul wrote in the epistle to the Romans (Rom 15:4), when it is read as the *living* word of God, then it will release its full message. The epistle to the Hebrews expressed brilliantly the effectiveness of the Old Testament:

> For the word of God is living and active, sharper than any two-edged sword, piercing to the division of soul and spirit, of joints and marrow, and discerning the thoughts and intentions of the heart (Heb 4:12).

We continue our study in the pages of this book, so that, again in the words of Vatican II, "easy access to sacred scripture should be provided for all the Christian faithful."

Chapter Two

Each Book, a Masterpiece

The proper method for reading the Bible comes naturally from the way that we meet a friend. A friend at times says something which we do not understand and perhaps something with which we do not agree. Often enough we let the matter drop, thinking to ourselves that our friend must have a reason for saying this or doing that, but we do not have the time nor the suitable occasion to discuss it. We do not allow this hidden or confusing situation to interfere with our friendship.

Our Friend, the Bible

Likewise with the Bible, we read statements which at first seem strange, even difficult, if not downright impossible to understand. Rather than impatiently close the Bible or, even worse, argue against it and ridicule it, we treat the Bible as we do a friend. We presume that God and the ancient Jewish writers had a reason for what they spoke and wrote. Sooner or later, with further time and study, we know that we will find out. About difficulties in the Bible, Pope Pius XII wrote:

> No one will be surprised if all difficulties are not yet solved and overcome; but even today serious problems greatly exercise the minds of Catholic exegetes. We should not lose courage on this account. . . . And if the wished-for solution is slow in coming or does not satisfy us, since perhaps a successful conclusion may be reserved to posterity, let us not wax impatient thereat.

. . . God wished difficulties to be scattered through the sacred Books inspired by him, in order that we might be urged to read and scrutinize them more intently, and, experiencing in a salutary manner our own limitations, we might be exercised in due submission of mind *(Divino Afflante Spiritu,* nn. 44–45).

Or if the Old Testament uses up page after page with lists of names, unpronounceable and unknown to us, as in Genesis, chapters 10–11 or in Numbers, chapters 1–3, or fills other pages with ceremonial laws completely out of touch with modern society, as often in the book of Leviticus, again we respond as to a friend.

Friends are always permitted to hang pictures of their relatives, completely unknown to us, to arrange their home, to cook and entertain, as it seems proper to them. Friends from other parts of the world will have ways of eating and entertaining that at first seem awkward and perhaps silly to us. Later we learn how wise they are in making the best use of their talents and property and in living peacefully and happily in their neighborhood.

As people of faith, we look upon the Bible not only as a friend but also as a word being spoken to us by God. This word comes from our all-wise creator, our most reliable confidant. We want to learn more about our friend and so we begin to look more closely at the Bible. In Chapter One of this book, we investigated the reasons prompting the editor to arrange the Bible as we find it in Jewish and Christian editions. Each, we saw, had a special purpose. Referring back to our earlier example, we recognize that our friends had good taste in arranging the various rooms in their home, the Bible.

We now look at two of these rooms, the two books of Exodus and Isaiah, to see if the same principle of appropriateness and good order applies. Continuing the same metaphor, we ask if the furniture in individual rooms of the house of the Bible is carefully put into place. Does each book of the Bible, like Exodus or Isaiah, show the touch of a master? Do the books communicate an attitude or insight about God's relation with Israel, the chosen people? The way that the sections are edited and stitched together speaks something unique which the individual parts by themselves would not have imparted to us. A chair, a table, a piece of cloth, a picture, a carpet—each has its own distinctive color, contour and beauty. Yet something new and lovely comes to our eye when we see them together in a room. Each object helps to bring out new aspects of beauty in the other, and the overall arrangement reveals the character of the family who lives in the home.

An Inspired and Living Tradition

Each home represents many generations with heirlooms, gifts, photos and most of all children with the traits of their ancestors. The Bible too represents several stages of divine inspiration. *First,* God was present with the people Israel, interiorly within their mind and heart, guiding and sustaining them. This initial inspiration was *seconded* and *affirmed* by another kind of divine impulsion. God raised up great leaders to speak and at times to write, people like Moses or Isaiah, to articulate what was unspoken in the hearts in all. A *third* stage is seen when disciples responded favorably and remembered what God had done or said through these leaders. *Finally,* lest these words and actions be forgotten, editors were inspired by God to collect and arrange what has now become a sacred tradition. These editors shared the faith and inspiration of the three previous stages.

The Catholic Church interprets the Bible in the same way that the Bible was inspired. The Bible does not stand alone, but as the word of God it lives within the community where God is present. God is particularly dwelling within the body of believers, the church. Paul writes:

> Do you not know that you are God's temple and that God's Spirit dwells in you? (1 Cor 3:16).

As the body of Christ, we the church consist of many members, each for a special purpose, again to quote Paul:

> Some should be apostles, some prophets, some evangelists, some pastors and teachers . . . for the work of the

ministry, for building up the body of Christ (Eph 4:11–12).

As "pastors and teachers" interpret and apply the Bible to daily life, an on-going, consistent body of tradition develops. The Bible receives its life from a living tradition, as in turn it directs that tradition forward.

We now investigate two books to see how editors drew upon ancient, inspired traditions to compose their work. One of these works, the book of Exodus, represents Israel's major piece of legislation, centering upon the covenant; the other, the book of Isaiah, gathers together prophetical responses to Israel's obedience or disobedience to God.

The Book of Exodus

"Exodus" is a Greek word, literally meaning "the way out of," in this case, the way out of Egypt toward the promised land. The book opens with the persecution of the children of Israel (chapters 1–2) and continues with Moses' interventions with Pharaoh, asking that the Israelites be permitted to leave Egypt (chapters 4–13). The journey from the borders of Egypt to Mount Sinai is then described (15:22–18:27), followed by three major pieces of legislation (chapters 20–23, 25–31, 35–39). Several key chapters have not been mentioned in this survey of the book of Exodus; we leave them aside for the moment.

Important religious truths already emerge from this outline, brief though it be. Israel did not possess the stamina and will to save itself. The people, like many other slaves, should have been lost to history within the sands of Egypt. Even in the wilderness, just three days after passing wondrously through the Red Sea, they wanted to return to Egypt. They murmured against Moses and his brother Aaron:

Would that we had died by the hand of the LORD in the land of Egypt, when we sat by the fleshpots and ate bread

to the full; for you have brought us into this wilderness
to kill this whole assembly with hunger (Ex 16:3).

God's response reveals another religious truth that supports and
pervades the entire Bible: God is to be known primarily as compassionate and forgiving. God cannot allow the people to remain
in slavery and will pardon their continuous flow of petty
grumbling.

Still another observation with serious consequences for the
study of the Bible comes to mind from scanning the book of
Exodus. Historical and geographical details turn out to be second-
ary. For instance, we are never told the name of the Pharaoh, nor
when he lived. The route taken by the Israelites and the location
of Mount Sinai are still disputed by archaeologists. St. Jerome
identified the mountain of the Lord at the oasis of Paran, to the
northwest of Mount Sinai. Obviously the purpose of the Bible is
not to prepare an historical document but a guide for worship and
instruction.

The Key to Organizing Exodus

We turn to the sections which were omitted in the earlier
survey of the book of Exodus. These chapters are crucial for
highlighting the important religious truths in Exodus, as we see
from their listing, italicized flush on the left-hand side of the
following schema:

1:1–2:25, Israel is oppressed in Egypt
3:1–4:17, God appears to Moses in the burning bush
4:18–13:22, Moses intercedes with Pharaoh
14:1–15:21, God leads Israel through the Red Sea
15:22–18:27, Difficulties in the desert
19:1–25, God appears to Moses atop Mount Sinai
20:1–23:33, covenant laws

24:1–18, God seals the covenant atop Mount Sinai
        25:1–31:18, ritual prescriptions
32:1–34:10, God renews the covenant atop Mount Sinai
        34:19–39:43, ritual prescriptions
40:1–38, God fills the meeting tent with glory

While the pages of the book of Exodus are filled mostly with narratives and laws, these are punctuated with marvelous interventions by God, as we see on the left-hand margin of the accompanying schema. We take each of these sections separately to see how they set the tone and attitude for the long series of laws and narratives in the book of Exodus. These sections are like spices and flavor in cooking, small in quantity compared to the food with which they are mixed, yet responsible for the success of the meal. Each of these interventions moves the story of Israel dramatically forward and lays a theological base to Israel's understanding of law.

In 3:1–4:17, God appears in a burning bush to Moses to summon him out of his peaceful existence in the land of Midian. Here he had married Zipporah, the daughter of the religious leader of the Midianites and with her had begotten two children. In chapter 3 God says to Moses from the burning bush:

> I have seen the affliction of my people who are in Egypt, and have heard their cry because of their taskmasters; I know their sufferings, and I have come down to deliver them out of the hand of the Egyptians and to bring them up out of that land to a good and broad land, a land flowing with milk and honey (Ex 3:7–8).

After 4:17 we follow Moses back to Egypt where he argues Israel's case before Pharaoh.

In 14:1–15:21 God's next great intervention happens. Israel has reached the Red Sea and once again was about to be swallowed into the sands of oblivion. The people recognized the hopelessness of their case, bitterly addressing Moses:

> Is it because there are no graves in Egypt that you have taken us away to die in the wilderness? What have you done to us, in bringing us out of Egypt? Is not this what we said to you in Egypt: "Let us alone and let us serve the Egyptians"? (Ex 14:11–12).

After the passage to the other side, out of danger from the Egyptians, first Moses and then his sister Miriam sing their canticle of praise and thanksgiving (Ex 15:1–21). Miriam's song was a refrain, to be sung over and over again:

> Sing to the LORD, gloriously triumphant, horse and rider
> the LORD has thrown into the sea (Ex 15:21, CS).

In the longer song Moses confesses his overpowering faith:

> The LORD is my strength and my song,
> the LORD has become my salvation (Ex 15:2).

This second of the short, major insertions in the book of Exodus is stating theologically that people do not, for they cannot, save themselves. Difficulties like those faced by Israel on the western shore of the Red Sea are insurmountable. Such indeed is the biblical symbolism of the sea, as in any number of passages (Pss 46:1–3; 89:10–11; Is 51:9–10; Mk 4:35–41). That fact, however, does not justify grumbling against God.

Yet Israel at once began to complain. Only three days after the glorious manifestation of God's power and concern at the Red Sea, the people murmured about the taste of the water (Ex 15:22–25) and about the scanty portions of bread (Ex 16). History repeats itself! After the next great appearance of God at Mount Sinai, we read:

> The Israelites lamented again, "Would that we had meat for food! We remember the fish we used to eat without cost in Egypt, and the cucumbers, the melons, the leeks,

> the onions, and the garlic. But now we are famished; we
> see nothing before us but this manna'' (Num 11:4–6).

In chapter 18 of Exodus human ways are sanctioned for handling
disputes and other problems among the people; the suggestion
came from Moses' father-in-law.

While the Bible points out that common sense is necessary,
nonetheless Israel stood in need of still greater wisdom. There
follows in the editing of the book of Exodus the next great intervention by God, this time at Mount Sinai. Atop this mountain God
appeared

> [amid] peals of thunder and lightning, and a heavy cloud
> over the mountain, and a very loud trumpet blast, so that
> all the people in the camp trembled. . . . Mount Sinai
> was all wrapped in smoke, for the LORD came down upon
> it in fire. The smoke rose from it as though from a fur-
> nace, and the whole mountain trembled violently
> (Ex 19:16).

In this awesome way the book of Exodus introduces the covenant
and its basic laws, found in chapters 20–23. Chapter 24 seals the
covenant with ritual acts atop Mount Sinai. Other prescriptions
for the ritual follow in chapters 25–31 and 35–39.

Much of this legal and ritual material is found outside the
Bible in ancient near eastern literature. These chapters of Exodus,
therefore, represent some of the best of human wisdom and culture. Centuries of human energy and experience have contributed to our Bible. Yet there is a difference between the Bible and
other ancient religions. The editor was very conscious that God
was transforming human wisdom into a new revelation of a personal, compassionate, faithful God. To communicate this new
appreciation of ancient wisdom, the editor stitched special,
highly religious sections into the narrative.

We continue to look at these all-important in-between sections which offer the context and frame, the light and depth, of
God's viewpoint on law and ritual.

In Exodus 19 Mount Sinai is wrapped in smoke, as the LORD descended upon it in fire. Moses goes up to God, and the LORD calls to him:

> Thus you shall say to the house of Jacob, and tell the people of Israel: "You have seen what I did to the Egyptians, and how I bore you on eagles' wings and brought you to myself. Now therefore, if you will obey my voice and keep my covenant, you shall be my own possession among all peoples . . . a kingdom of priests and a holy nation" (vv. 3–6).

Theologically Israel does not become God's elect people by any personal merit—an idea quickly dismissed in Deuteronomy 7:6–11—but by God's generous, loving choice.

In Exodus 24 Moses again climbs the mountain, covered with the glory of the Lord and a dense cloud. We are then told:

> The appearance of the glory of the LORD was like a devouring fire. . . . Moses entered the cloud . . . and was on the mountain forty days and forty nights (vv. 15–18).

The important religious message is being communicated about laws and ritual. It is not enough to read them in a legal document nor to obey them blindly. Like Moses we need to hear them as spoken by God and prayerfully to consider their purpose and effect. Throughout, we pray and study with the faith that God is guiding us and receiving our obedience and worship.

In Exodus chapter 32 Moses is again on the mountain, only to come down and find the people in sinful revelry. He smashes the tablets of the law (chapter 32). He realizes that people, even those who received the covenant and its laws amid the glorious theophany of Mount Sinai, cannot live by laws alone. Moses desires to reach beyond all human situations, even those most sacred, and to look upon the face of God (chapter 33). God replies that no one "sees me and still lives" (Ex 33:20).

God returns to the original idea of a covenant and the need of

laws. After summoning Moses again to the summit of Mount Sinai,
the Lord passes by. As Moses holds the two tablets of the laws in
his arms, God calls out:

> The LORD, the LORD, a God merciful and gracious, slow
> to anger, and abounding in steadfast love and faithful-
> ness (Ex 34:6).

Again it is clear that laws, as recorded in chapters 20–23 and
ritual in chapters 25–31 and 35–39, cannot by themselves maintain the holiness of Israel. They must be interpreted and obeyed
in the vision of a gracious, merciful and faithful God. In chapter
one we discussed the need to shift the emphasis from the WORD of
God to the word of GOD, from study to prayer. Now we recognize
that the emphasis must be nuanced still more carefully. We do not
listen to the word of GOD but to the word of God COMPASSIONATE
AND FAITHFUL.

When Moses came down from the mount, his skin was trans-
lucent from the glory of the Lord. Thereafter, he wore a veil over
his face unless he was speaking with God in prayer.

Finally in Exodus 40, the last chapter of Exodus, the editor
prepares for the laws and ritual in the books of Leviticus and
Numbers. Moses will no longer be with the people nor on hand to
ascend the mountain of the Lord for conversation with God. After
Moses carefully prepares the meeting tent for worship, "the
cloud covered the tent of meeting, and the glory of the LORD filled
the tabernacle." The wonder of Mount Sinai is being transferred
to the meeting tent and future temple. Yet not even Moses could
enter such a wondrous place. Even this most holy of all persons
was himself subject to God. The implication is also given that the
words of Moses, in the sacred tablets and books, contain a mystery
beyond human comprehension.

The book of Exodus does not end with this mystical, almost
impossible situation, where God is beyond reach. Instead, we are
told in the very last verses:

> Throughout all their journeys, whenever the cloud was
> taken up from over the tabernacle, the people of Israel
> would go onward; but if the cloud was not taken up,

then they did not go onward till the day that it was taken
up. For throughout all their journeys the cloud of the
LORD was upon the tabernacle by day, and fire was in it
by night, in the sight of all the house of Israel (Ex
40:36–38).

Israel and ourselves as the new Israel are given the promise that
God will always be with us, directing our activity day by day and
night by night. Laws and ritual, even the sacred meeting tent or
temple, were not able by themselves to maintain Israel in grace
and justice. The people must live, moment by moment, in the
presence of God, carefully guiding them and continuously solic-
iting their love and loyalty.

The editing of the book of Exodus, accordingly, joins exceptional human effort with superhuman, divine presence. The best
which humankind is capable of is given to God, to be permeated
with a divine spirit. Thus the details and plans are cleansed and
purified, rearranged and redirected. Exodus is not a book of what
happened once and never again. It becomes a model of life for
each new generation of Israelites and for us today.

The Book of Isaiah

We turn now to another book of the Old Testament as an
example of editing earlier material. The preaching and writing of
a person inspired by God, whose name was Isaiah, were received
by disciples who shared in that inspiration and kept the message
alive amid new generations of Israelites. These too were people
of faith, also inspired by God to live holy, noble lives. There was
continuity, but continuity meant adaptation to new circumstances of life.

Several important insights occur to us from the previous
paragraph. Inspiration is shared by different groups of individuals: for instance, the prophet Isaiah, his disciples, the people
Israel. All are moved by God, but what is a generic hope among
the people becomes a clear message in the mind and on the lips of
the prophet. What is a very creative moment for the prophet turns
into faithful, creative repetition by the disciples. For this reason,

we speak of an *inspired tradition.* To know what God is saying to us in the book of Isaiah requires a sense of this long history of the Isaian tradition.

First we observe a major difference between the book of Exodus and that of Isaiah. Exodus represents the most basic, fundamental bedrock of Israel's life. Exodus provides us with the themes that become central to the Bible: liberation from Egypt, covenant at Mount Sinai, an elect people, promise of land and freedom for worshiping God, assurance of God's continual guidance.

The book of Isaiah begins some five hundred years later. In the first part of Isaiah (chapters 1–39), the exodus out of Egypt has been eclipsed by God's enthronement in the Jerusalem temple. The mount of the Lord is no longer Sinai but the place of the temple (Is 2:2–5). The covenant and the temple have been entrusted to the Davidic kings to safeguard.

The book of Isaiah represents a major endeavor to deal with all of these major religious themes. In the midst of mammoth changes, and in view of still more shattering changes to come, the editor seems to be asking: Is God faithful and dependable? Is God still present with Israel? Are God's promises still true? Beginning with the preaching of the great prophet of Jerusalem, Isaiah son of Amoz (Is 1:1), the editor answers these questions:

in part one, chapters 1–39, while the city of Jerusalem and its temple, its kings and nobles, were still in place;

in part two, chapters 40–55, when all these institutions, once endowed with eternal, divine promises, are destroyed and the people are scattered in exile throughout the Babylonian empire;

in part three, chapters 56–66, after some of the people have returned from exile and are seeking to reconstruct their life, this time without Davidic kings and national pride, exclusively within Jerusalem and its temple.

The book of Isaiah embraces a long stretch of time, from 750 to 500 B.C. It represents a gigantic effort:

first to purify and revitalize what has become soiled and stale (chapters 1–39);

then to comfort and prepare for the new age during the exile and its time of purification and suffering (chapters 40–55);

finally, to critique the dismal small-mindedness of the people after their return from exile and eventually to look beyond the present moment for the new heavens and the new earth (chapters 56–66).

Israel would hardly have survived such traumatic shocks to its faith and life had there not been an inspired Isaiah with creative insights, a series of inspired disciples with realistic adaptations, an inspired people who despite their weakness and fear realized in their heart that God was with them through it all. Inspiration again is a long tradition of godly people, each acting and reacting in different ways. We look to see how disciples held this tradition together in the book of Isaiah.

(a) *The prophet Isaiah* preached between 750 and 692 B.C. He was strong and self-confident (1:18–20), large-minded and exceptionally talented (2:2–5), reliant upon faith (7:9), even though faced with rejection (6:9–10; 7:10–12; 31:1).

(b) *The first disciples* appear when persecution and rejection cast doubts upon the continuity of Isaiah's message. Someone must carry it on. We read:

> Bind up the testimony, seal the teaching among my disciples. I will wait for the LORD, who is hiding his face from the house of Jacob, and I will hope in this God. Behold, I and the children whom the LORD has given me are signs and portents to Israel from the LORD of hosts, who dwells on Mount Zion [i.e., Jerusalem] (Is 8:16–18).

(c) *The preaching is written down,* partially by Isaiah and partially by disciples. Impending disaster could obliterate the memory as it did destroy the temple, city and Davidic dynasty:

> And now, go, write it before them on a tablet,
>   and inscribe it in a book,
> that it may be for the time to come
>   as a witness for ever.

> For they are a rebellious people,
>   lying sons and daughters,
> sons and daughters who will not hear
>   the instruction of the Lord (Is 30:8–9, CS).

(d) *Another disciple during the exile* in a foreign land (587–529 B.C.) carries all of these burdens yet with hope for the future in a just, faithful God:

> The LORD God has given me
>   the tongue of those who are taught,
> that I may know how to sustain with a word
>   those who are weary.
> Morning by morning God wakens,
>   wakens my ear
>   to hear as those who are taught.
> The LORD God has opened my ear (Is 50:4–5).

The phrase, "those who are taught" translates a single Hebrew word which is also used with the meaning "disciple." Discipleship means: fidelity to the people Israel, even to carrying the burden of their suffering and guilt; fidelity to Isaiah, whose message, nonetheless, must be adapted to an entirely new situation, away from Jerusalem in a foreign land; and most of all, fidelity to God who wakens the ear to listen and to learn in the way that disciples are taught.

(e) *Finally, discipleship continues in the years after the exile when the people are back again in Jerusalem.* In a passage that has strong resemblance to 50:4–9, we read:

> The Spirit of the LORD is upon me,
>   because the LORD has anointed me
> to bring good tidings to the afflicted;
>   God has sent me to bind up the brokenhearted (Is 61:1).

This passage is recognized at once as that chosen by Jesus to begin his own prophetic ministry at Nazareth (Lk 4:16–22). The continuity carries on with the prophetic mantle on the shoulders of Jesus.

With this background in mind, that the book of Isaiah is a long, inspired prophetic tradition, sustained and adapted over several centuries by faithful disciples, we examine the book to see how the final editor put it all together.

Part One: Threats of Destruction and Exile

Chapters 1–12. Oracles on Judah and Jerusalem, the quintessence of Isaiah's preaching, which itself can be subdivided: *chapter 1,* grand opening, threatening Jerusalem with almost total destruction; *chapters 2–5,* the earliest preaching of the prophet with its own introduction (2:1–5); *chapters 6–12,* frequently called, "The Book of Immanuel," because of the famous prophecy in 7:14. The initial account about the call of the prophet is delayed till chapter 6, as an encouragement against the repudiation in chapters 2–5.

Chapters 13–23. The disciples have extended the oracles to include all the nations of the world.

Chapters 24–27. The scope now reaches the heavens and the earth, the entire cosmos.

Chapters 28–33. Some of Isaiah's oracles which were passed over in the earlier collection of chapters 1–12 are preserved here, with more serious consequences not only for Judah but also for the world.

Chapters 34–35. The editor rounds out the theme of destruction in chapters 28–33, with hope for a return from exile.

Chapters 36–39. The grand appendix, drawn mostly from 2 Kings 18:13–20:19, again repeating the threat of Judah's destruction and the scattering of the people in exile, thus preparing for the following section.

Part Two: Consolation and Atonement

Chapters 40–55. During Israel's exile in the Babylonian empire a new disciple sings hauntingly of the purifying power of suffering and of the new exodus from foreign lands to their homeland.

Part Three: Disappointment and New Hopes

Chapters 56–66. During the discouraging years after the return from exile, the disciples pray for the new heavens and the new earth.

The sixty-six chapters of Isaiah span an enormous stretch of years, geography and themes: from 750 to 500; from Jerusalem to Babylon and back again to Jerusalem; from city, temple and dynasty to their chaotic destruction; across the cosmos to new heavens and a new earth. Yet they are stitched together by key words about justice and by a religious struggle to accept a universal scope in God's promises.

Synonyms for justice occur over and over again. In the Bible "justice" means much more than duly punishing sins or properly giving what a person deserves. Justice includes the idea of reaching the norm set by God for the chosen people, and, more mysteriously still, the insight that God will always be just in fulfilling the divine promises. The opening chapter begins with a lawsuit where the courtroom is the world. Chapters 40–55 argue repeatedly in favor of God's faithfulness in fulfilling all promises, most eloquently in chapter 48. Some of the most extensive discussions of justice, human and divine, are found in chapters 58–59 within the third major section of the book of Isaiah.

The editor of this magnificent body of prophetic traditions does not turn back from announcing the destruction of Jerusalem and the toppling of the Davidic dynasty, whatever may have been the eternal promises invested in them earlier in the Bible, as in Psalms 46 and 132. Out of this destruction will come a still more glorious realization of what God really has in mind. This topic comes up again in this book while discussing messianic hopes in chapter six.

With the benefit of time, the editor also saw how God wrote straight with crooked lines in still another way. The foreign nations, the instrument for Israel's destruction (Is 10:5), become so involved in God's plans for Israel's salvation that they receive a share in that salvation. Each of the major sections concludes (and sometimes begins) with a positive word for the nations: see 12:5–6; 23:17–18; 27:13; 33:17–24; 35:10; 40:4 and 55:3–5; 56:1–8 and 66:18–24.

The disciples and editor gave this exceptionally complex body of prophetical tradition a rather clear focus, in order to invite the people Israel to their missionary vocation toward the world. The book of Isaiah not only keeps Israel faithful to their Mosaic heritage, but it also expands that heritage in ways never dreamed of by Moses.

Conclusion

True, many details were introduced into this explanation of the books of Exodus and Isaiah. Yet, much of this enterprise could have been done even by a first reader of the Bible. The principles for this way of studying the Bible advise us:

first, read the Bible just as it is, but read it as a friend, always giving it the benefit of the doubt that the editor had a reason for everything;

second, read the Bible, to detect the overall plan or organization within individual books. Seek to determine what are the principal themes within each section of the book and what are the links holding all the sections together. These links generally reveal the major theological purpose of the editor;

third, read the Bible with an eye for the way that normal human resources, plans and activities are drawn into a larger, deeper divine plan. God thus uplifts and transforms, all the while faithfully fulfilling the hidden hopes within us from creation.

The inspiration which we meet in the Bible begins with an exceptionally gifted, saintly *individual,* like a Moses or an Isaiah, inspired by God to legislate, preach and write as well as to lead the people forward. These leaders had a *group of followers and disciples,* inspired less for creativity, more for continuity and application to later circumstances. Finally, another individual, the *editor,* was inspired to draw together the long tradition into a single book. Throughout this process the community of Israel was inspired, but in ways more generic and less forceful than was the case with creative individuals like Moses or Isaiah, their disciples and editors. Biblical inspiration includes all of these "inspirations."

Last of all, reading and praying the Bible today within the larger community of the church enable us to share the way in which the Bible was inspired long ago.

Chapter Three

Assembling for Worship and Instruction

In chapters one and two of this book we came to realize how carefully the Old Testament was put together, not only in its sequence of books but also in the arrangement within individual books. Time after time, we recognize the hand of a genius at work, intent not only to bring the best of human ingenuity to the task, but also to allow these human talents to be transformed by God's marvelous direction. Inspiration is the name for this intervention and grace from God. We now seek out the place or the setting which these dedicated, inspired people found most compatible for their work.

The Creative Moment of Sanctuary Worship

The largest part of the Bible, we propose, originated amid community prayer and preaching. Instructions and sermons, prayers and songs, rubrics and laws were necessary to direct and enrich Israel's assemblies of worship. At times religious leaders gathered this material together. These collections were preserved more often than not in "memory books." They were inscribed as written documents, generally at times of crisis (as in the days of Jeremiah: see Jer 36) or during a vigorous, religious reform (as undertaken by Kings Hezekiah and Josiah: see 2 Chr 29–31, 34–35). Whether as "memory" or "written" books, the Bible was gradually evolving and taking the shape that it is today. We should repeat that this entire process was under the inspiration of the Holy Spirit. Inspiration, therefore, was a grace shared by many persons in many different ways.

This norm of viewing the Bible as material created for worship, we hasten to add, must be applied discreetly. Some parts of the Old Testament, like Proverbs and Ecclesiastes, were not composed for formal liturgy at all. Yet even these sections may have been used for the instruction of youths which often took place as families gathered at Jerusalem or some other important shrine for religious and social festivities (cf. Dt 6:20–25; 26:1–11; Neh 8–10). Still other parts of the Old Testament probably emerged spontaneously at the evening campfire for entertainment, like the stories of the judge Ehud (Jgs 3:12–30) or of the heroic warrior Samson (Jgs 13–16). Such entertainment was normal as people gathered for the pilgrimage festivals. Without radio, TV or cinemas, singers and story tellers provided live coverage.

To appreciate the wide complex of life at the central sanctuaries and at the Jerusalem temple, it is well to recall how different these places were from Christian churches. In a country like Israel with a long dry season, from late March to early November, "temple" or "sanctuary" consisted of a large, open square, generally on a hilltop, at the center of which was a small shrine where only the highest dignitaries of priesthood and royalty ever entered. The courtyard was used not only for sacred services like sacrifice, prayer and singing, but also for instruction, for rest and quiet relaxation, and on the outer edge for picnic meals and sleep. Here at the "temple" or "sanctuary" all of life converged around God's presence in the shrine.

Sanctuaries occupy an ever more important role in our study, once we realize that most of the narratives in the Old Testament center their events at famous places of worship. Places like Bethel, Shechem, Gilgal, Beer-sheba and Jerusalem come repeatedly into the biblical story. For instance, when Abraham enters the promised land (Gen 12:6–8), when Jacob as a young man prepares to leave for Haran to avoid the anger of Esau (Gen 28:10–22) or as an old man brings his entire family to Egypt (Gen 46:1), sanctuaries occupy center stage for the important events.

The Old Testament often leaves the impression that its narratives are placed within a framework of sanctuary hymns. Genesis begins and ends with a hymn or blessing (Gen 1 and 49) and the book of Exodus with God's appearances at a sacred place (Ex 3 and 40). Deuteronomy closes with sanctuary blessings and services (Dt 26–34); the two books of Samuel place the canticle of Hannah at the beginning (1 Sam 2) and that of David toward the end (2 Sam 22). Quite often the prophetical books are so edited that a short hymn occurs at the beginning (Is 2:2–5; Am 1:2; Mi 1:2–4; Nah 1:2–8) or at the end (Hab 3) while the second major part of Isaiah (chapters 40–55) moves with the rhythm and vocabulary of sacred melodies. More than anything else, the Bible carries the label: "made for worship."

The statement has already been made, and these details further reinforce its truthfulness: the *purpose* of the Bible is not to describe ancient events with detailed accuracy but rather from the memory of the events to draw listeners into worshiping God and into reliving the hopes of the ancestors.

This fact helped to produce several key words in the book of Deuteronomy: for instance, *this day* or *today,* and *we who are alive,* as in the passage:

> And Moses summoned all Israel and said to them, "Hear, O Israel, the statutes and the ordinances which I speak *in your hearing this day,* and you shall learn them and be careful to do them. The LORD our God made a covenant *with us* in Horeb. Not with our ancestors did the LORD make this covenant, but *with us,* who are *all of us here alive this day . . ."* (Dt 5:1–3).

We take note of the setting: *hear* (not to read) at a place of assembly; *apply* to the people's lives, so as to *be careful to do them;* do it *this day;* have a sense of the covenant's being renewed *with us, all of us here alive this day.*

Early Events in Later Preaching

The Bible continuously interacts with events on planet earth, especially in the history of Israel. Yet its main intention is not to record events and write a history book. Otherwise, it would have provided important details like the name of the Pharaoh who accepted the family of Jacob into Egypt and gave Joseph the highest honor in the land; or the name of the other Pharaoh who oppressed the Israelites; or the time when these persons lived. Ancient chroniclers normally recorded such central historical details on temple walls; their accounts were succinct but detailed. The Bible, therefore, has a different kind of history writing, that of stories (a practice shared with other peoples in the ancient near east), but there is still a difference in how the Bible appreciates the main actor, "the LORD your God, who brought you out of the land of Egypt" (Ex 20:2).

The problem of the *Bible and history* shows up in still another way. Archaeologists have uncovered and deciphered a voluminous amount of material from what is called the new kingdom in Egypt, particularly in the case of the great warrior and temple builder, Ramses II (1290–1224 B.C.). He is the most likely candidate for the oppressor of the Israelites who forced them into slave labor for his grandiose constructions. Yet, not a word about Israel is found in any of Ramses' monuments. Ramses II's successor, Merneptah (1224–1211 B.C.), provides the solitary mention of Israel in ancient Egyptian documents. Merneptah's tablet, now in the Cairo museum, lists Israel, not as a city or kingdom, but as a people whom his army encountered during a campaign into Palestine. If the Bible was intending to provide us with an adequate historical account, then a few salient dates and names would have been apropos and much appreciated by archaeologists and historians. The ten plagues (Ex 7–12), which the Bible claims to have devastated every aspect of Egyptian life—in the homes, in the temple, in the farmlands and work places—should have been acknowledged somewhere in the tons of Egyptian documentation at our disposal. Yet not a whisper about them!

Again, it is not that the Bible is wrong but that it was adapting the memory of original events to the living conditions of later ages which an effective preacher needs to consider. Put very simply, the accounts of the plagues in Exodus 7–12, as well as in Psalms 78:40–51, 105:28–38; Wisdom 11–12 and 17–18, all homilize or draw instruction and application for later generations. Each wants to insist that wherever persons sin, there the plague strikes to turn their light to darkness, their sweetness to bitterness. The rhetoric of a brilliant preacher shows up as we compare two accounts of the first plague, that of turning water into blood. We put them side by side: on the *left* what is called the Yahwist tradition, an earlier style of narrative; on the *right,* the Priestly tradition, a later form of instruction and preaching:

Yahwist	*Priestly*
Moses is to say to Pharaoh: "I will strike the water that is in the Nile with the rod that is in my hand, and it shall be turned to blood. . . . All the Egyptians *dug about the Nile for water to drink.*"	Say to Aaron, "Take your rod and stretch out your hand over the waters of Egypt, over their rivers, their canals, and their ponds, and all their pools of water, that they may become blood, and there shall be *blood throughout all the land of Egypt, both in vessels of wood and in vessels of stone.*"

If the Priestly tradition weaves in various rhetorical flourishes—water everywhere, even in vessels of wood and stone (more literally, the sap in trees and the water from rocky springs), it all turned into blood—the preacher never intended to falsify the records. The orator was not correcting the "J" or Yahwist tradition which more modestly claimed that only the River Nile was turned into blood, so that water was still available, albeit at some inconvenience, from springs and wells. Rather the homilist was seeking to move the later generation to realize that if they sin, everything they touch or possess will be polluted and unusable.

The Basic Rubric

While relying upon real events, the inspired authors of the Bible did not intend to write history but to lead later generations of people in worship and instruction. The following rubric attempts to express the steps in the formation of the Bible.

(a) Real events, insignificant at the time for the secular chronicler of world history, set Israel apart from other people as God's chosen ones.

(b) Israel celebrates the memory of these events which become central to worship and instruction.

(c) As worship draws ever larger numbers of people into celebrating and reliving the event, the original event takes on ever larger proportions in the people's lives. Liturgy requires songs and narratives, creeds and instructions, religious acts like processions, sacrifice of animals and agricultural products, sacred meals. Within these liturgical needs, the Bible begins to take shape.

(d) Because of the impact of liturgical celebrations in forming a strong, fervent Israel, other nations, like Egypt, Assyria and Babylon, have to deal with Israel, as today must the atheistic government of Soviet Russia. The real but insignificant event of long ago *now* becomes "historical," impacting the world of politics and economics. It is remembered more for the way it is celebrated than for the way it happened.

History, therefore, requires something more than that an event happened; the event must have repercussions on a large scale. To take a down-to-earth example: most probably each of us, after rising from bed and eating breakfast this morning, brushed our teeth. Even if we are a world celebrity, this real event will never make history! The crucifixion of Jesus just by itself would not have been recorded in history books; many people were crucified by the Romans and forgotten. It was the *remembrance* of Jesus' death and resurrection, particularly through eucharistic celebration but also through the instructions in the gospels, that Jesus' death *became* historical.

What the Bible presents primarily is liturgical celebration and religious instruction. These sought to involve each new generation. Liturgy, accordingly, makes history out of events that never would have qualified for history. Liturgy puts an aura of faith and wonder around the original event, so as to draw the worshiper into a stance of prayer and praise. Liturgy intends to sensitize the worshiper to God's continuous presence in daily life, and thus to bring out the hidden potential of life. Liturgy activates earthly life with heavenly repercussions.

In order that the earlier, insignificant event may become history, liturgy itself must meet certain conditions. Unless liturgical celebrations interact with important aspects of life—for instance, with hunger and homelessness, with social injustices, with drought and other natural disasters, with disease and serious medical problems, with motivation for peace and good morals—liturgy will exert little or no influence and leave nothing behind but its aura of stale incense and ceilings darkened with candle smoke. The exodus out of Egypt and the crucifixion of Jesus left their marks on history and thereby became historical, because they sustained the hopes of new generations of people in their own bondage and indignities. Little wonder that liberation theology turns to these important moments in the Bible.

We now look at several important aspects of assembly worship, to attune ourselves to the setting for the composition and editing of the biblical books.

The Sanctuary at Shechem

Important liturgical passages, like Deuteronomy 27–33 and Joshua 23–24, are explicitly linked with the sacred town of Shechem. Other chapters, like Deuteronomy 26, may also witness to the religious services at the Shechem sanctuary. No description or commentary can replace the stirring eloquence of these chapters. The orator throws the gauntlet down and demands a decision for the God of the covenant.

> I call heaven and earth to witness against you this day [again, the insistence of Deuteronomy upon "this day"], that I have set before you life and death, blessing and curse; therefore choose life, that you and your descendants may live, loving the LORD your God, obeying his voice, and cleaving to him (Dt 30:19–20).

In Joshua 24 a dramatic interchange takes place between the people and Joshua or the liturgical presider:

> *Joshua:* If you be unwilling to serve the LORD, choose this day [once again, the theme of "this day"] whom you will serve. . . . But as for me and my house, we will serve the LORD.
>
> *People:* Far be it from us that we should forsake the LORD, to serve other gods. . . . We will serve the LORD.
>
> *Joshua:* You cannot serve the LORD; for he is a holy God . . . a jealous God.
>
> *People:* Nay; but we will serve the LORD.
>
> *Joshua:* You are witnesses against yourselves that you have chosen the LORD, to serve him.
>
> *People:* We are witnesses.
>
> *Joshua:* Then put away the foreign gods . . . and incline your heart to the LORD, the God of Israel.
>
> *People:* The LORD our God we will serve, and his voice we will obey.
>
> *Narrator:* So Joshua wrote these words in the book of the law of God, and he took a great stone, and set it up there under the oak in the sanctuary of the Lord.
>
> *Joshua:* Behold, this stone shall be a witness against us; for it has heard all the words of the LORD which he spoke to us; therefore it shall be a witness against you, lest you deal falsely with your God.
>
> *Narrator:* So Joshua sent the people away, every person to their inheritance.

Other aspects of Israel's worship show up in the song of Moses in Deuteronomy 32 and in the blessing upon the tribes in Deuteronomy 33. These passages provide a summary of biblical history. This overview of what God has done for the people from the time of Abraham and Sarah or at least from the lifetime of Moses turns into a classic statement of Israel's creed in Deuteronomy 26:5–10 and Joshua 24:2–13. Like the Apostles' Creed and the Nicene Creed, professed by Catholics at all Sunday masses, these in the Old Testament consist almost exclusively of God's marvelous actions as savior in the historical setting of people's lives. We easily picture the Israelite people, as a family or village community, standing before the priest at the sanctuary and declaring:

> A wandering Aramean was my father; and he went down into Egypt and sojourned there, few in number; and there he became a nation, great, mighty, and populous. And the Egyptians treated us harshly, and afflicted us, and laid upon us hard bondage. Then we cried to the LORD the God of our ancestors, and the LORD heard our voice, and saw our affliction, our toil, and our oppression; and the LORD brought us out of Egypt with a mighty hand and an outstretched arm, with great terror, with signs and wonders; and he brought us into this place and gave us this land, a land flowing with milk and honey. And behold, now I bring the first of the fruit of the ground, which thou, o LORD, hast given me (Dt 26:5–10).

We note once more the contemporaneity of this statement of faith, through the use of such words as "us" and "we," "this place" and "this land." The ancestors identify themselves completely with the later congregation; the later generations take ownership of the sufferings and difficulties of their forebears in Egypt. In reliving them, they are in fact very conscious of the religious spirit which motivated the first event: God's all powerful, compassionate concern for people in serious trouble. This attitude of faith, more than the details of the earlier event, survives intact.

This summary of Israel's history would have occasioned the need of further explanation. Hence there arose the longer narratives which gradually became the books of Genesis through Deuteronomy.

The book of Deuteronomy ends with the story of Moses' death. God brought him to the top of Mount Nebo, on the eastern side of the river Jordan, to view the entire promised land, as far north as Dan, as far west as the Great Sea, as far south as the desert wilderness of the Negeb. God then said:

> I have let you feast your eyes upon it, but you shall not
> go over there (Dt 34:4).

There Moses, the greatest of the prophets and the servant of the Lord, died. His grave was never found. Rather Israel was to search for Moses in his legacy of the covenant and its laws. Somehow or other Israel was always to be on the other side of the Jordan, about to take up where Moses left off, seeking ways to be more worthy of this beautiful land, flowing with milk and honey, more deserving of the children born to them in this land.

The entire five books of Moses were thus their history and their future, their instruction and their life. Israel, therefore, must listen over and over again to its story in the story of Genesis through Deuteronomy. For this reason, even in the synagogue today, when the lector comes to the end of Deuteronomy in the yearly cycle of reading the five books of Moses, the lector never stops with Deuteronomy 34:12 but begins at once with Genesis 1:1. The reading of the Torah must never end but is always beginning over again. The reliving of the founding days of creation (Gen 1–11), of the initial revelations to the patriarchs (Gen 12–50), and of the work of Moses (Ex, Lev, Num, Dt) continues into the lives of each new generation. The day when the reading of Deuteronomy 34:12 flows over into Genesis 1:1 has become one of Israel's most joyful festivals, called the feast of *simhat ha-torah*, "the joy of the Torah." Such joy can never be muffled, and for us Christians it leads into eternity through another Moses, whom we venerate as Jesus Christ.

The Jerusalem Assembly Under Ezra

We said that the children of Israel each year were positioning themselves spiritually on the other side of the river Jordan, overlooking the promised land and waiting to (re-)enter it. They annually reviewed their obedience to the hopes and expectations of God as expressed through Moses. Despite the warnings of the prophets and despite the great religious renewals under King Hezekiah (2 Kgs 18–20; 2 Chr 29–31) and King Josiah (2 Kgs 22–23; 2 Chr 34–35), the people continued in their rebellious lack of faith and eventually were driven off their land into exile, scattered across the Babylonian empire (modern Iraq into Syria and Lebanon).

God again heard their cries of pain and brokenness; God delivered them from their foreign bondage and brought them back to their promised land. Prophets such as Haggai and Zechariah stirred them out of their lethargy to rebuild the temple. Another prophet, Joel, called for a solemn fast, so that they would be delivered from a locust plague and again focus their eyes upon a vision of peace and abundance. Again the people at Jerusalem lapsed into mediocre devotion toward God and into social sins of easy divorce, and again God raised up a prophet, this time Malachi, who turns the dismal darkness into an announcement of the messianic age. And again they sinned.

Their story is the story of all of us. And like Israel we stand in need of the vigorous reformer, Ezra, who appeared upon the scene in 428 B.C. and reshaped Israel into the kind of people whom we know today as Jews. Ezra is frequently called the father of Judaism, the new Moses.

The great reform of Ezra is told for us in the book under his name (chapters 7–10) and in the book of Nehemiah (chapters 8–13). A quick walk through these chapters will attune us to the way in which the Bible, especially the five books of Moses, reached a final shape. From then onward the text was generally kept intact. Instead of absorbing new aspects of sanctuary worship, they became the subject of interpretation. No longer would the explanations and applications of the priests and scribes be incorporated into the text, as happened earlier, but would be part of tradition, accompanying the text in worship and religious instruction.

We observe these stages in the assembly called by Ezra to inaugurate his reform:

> All the people gathered as one person into the square before the Water Gate; and they told Ezra the scribe to

bring the book of the law of Moses which the LORD had given to Israel.

After providing a wooden platform for himself and surrounding himself with the leaders of the people, he read from it . . . from early morning until midday, in the presence of the men and the women and those who could understand; and the ears of all the people were attentive to the book of the law.

The reading of the law is surrounded with impressive ceremony:

Ezra opened the book in the sight of all the people, for he was above all the people, and when he opened it all the people stood. And Ezra blessed the LORD, the great God, and all the people answered, "Amen, Amen," lifting up their hands; and they bowed their heads, and worshiped the LORD with their faces to the ground.

An important comment follows in this chapter 8 of the book of Nehemiah:

The Levites helped the people to understand the law, while the people remained in their places. And they read from the book, from the law of God, clearly; and they gave the sense, so that the people understood the reading.

Many other liturgical and moral prescriptions follow: the construction of booths from tree branches joyfully to relive the days of Moses, and Ezra's reading the law and instructing the people during an octave (Neh 8:13–18); a day of fasting on the twenty-fourth day of the month with further instruction (Neh 9: 1–5); a long review or creed of Israel's sacred history (Neh 9: 6–37); the reform of morals (Neh 10); repeopling Jerusalem (Neh 11); the duties and rights of the priests and Levites (Neh

12); rules for the temple, for the sabbath and for marriage
(Neh 13).

Many scholars place here during this great reform of Ezra the
final editing of the five books of Moses and the beginning of two
other important facets of Israel's religious life. The phrase about
reading the law of God *clearly, giving the sense, so that the
people understood,* may refer to the targums and to midrashic
and other writings. "Targum" was a translation of the Bible into
Aramaic, the vernacular language spoken by the people upon
their return from exile. "Midrash" was a style of interpreting
scripture, first by quoting the relevant passage and then letting
the passage blend into the contemporary age of the speaker. Similar to midrash is still another form of literature called "hagga-
dah," stories which did not necessarily quote scripture but wove
biblical allusions into its text.

These new kinds of biblically related material never remained locked into the ancient historical setting of a Bible text,
nor did they quote the scripture with absolute literalness. Adaptations and explanations were continuously being woven into the
original passage. One example from Isaiah 19:25 may help us to
understand the targum. We should keep in mind that still other
forms of interpretation were even freer in their re-reading of the
Hebrew text.

Hebrew Text	*Aramaic Targum*
Blessed be Egypt my people, and Assyria the work of my hands, and Israel my inheritance.	Blessed are my people whom I brought forth from Egypt; because they sinned against me I exiled them to Assyria. And now that they repent they are called my people and my heritage Israel.

Evidently the more universal approach toward the foreign
nations in the Hebrew text was judged inappropriate at a later
age. At a synagogal service the Hebrew *text* was carefully *read.* It
was followed by the targum, an *oral* rendition into the *vernacu-*

lar. In the case of Isaiah 19:25 each rendering is theologically correct, but the Hebrew text is more open to foreigners, while the Aramaic version remained more cautious. The change is due to pastoral judgment: what would be more helpful for Jewish people to be true to the covenant and to live at peace with their neighbors.

Conclusion

We delayed over two great assemblies of Israel, one at an early stage, the second at a late point in Israelite history. The assembly at Shechem, as recorded in Deuteronomy, helps to map the lines of development in the formation of the five books of Moses. The assembly at Jerusalem under the leadership of the scribe Ezra represents another crucial transition in biblical religion. While Deuteronomy enables us to see the Mosaic traditions still in development, Ezra shows us a different kind of development after the written text is finalized.

Each assembly stresses the central place given to *oral transmission.* The Mosaic text was being *heard, explained,* and *applied.* The text, therefore, was always accompanied by tradition. The text was the heart of tradition; tradition for its part became the legs, hands and eyes of the text. The text supplied the lifeblood; the tradition brought that life into new settings, where new hopes and new problems were faced.

If time and space permitted, many more assemblies could be studied to reinforce the positions of this chapter. The great reforms of King Hezekiah (2 Kgs 18–20; 2 Chr 29–32) and especially of King Josiah (2 Kgs 22–23; 2 Chr 34–35) were crucial for preserving earlier traditions. These texts integrated the Mosaic heritage with later adaptations up to the time of Hezekiah and Josiah.

Chapter one of this book looked at the entire Old Testament, chapter two at individual books. Each showed the hand of a loyal, brilliant theologian in the work of editing and arrangement. Single books and the whole corpus of books were keeping the ancient revelation alive in new periods of Israel's life. Chapter three has shown that the vitality to undertake this work came principally from the sanctuary and most especially from the people at prayer and worship.

The liturgy of the church performs the same service for us. The church has arranged what can be called "a liturgical Bible." This work is found in the lectionary where the entire Bible is read on a three year cycle on Sundays, on a two year cycle on weekdays. The liturgy as revised and reformed through the influence of the Second Vatican Council integrates various biblical passages with the seasons of the year (i.e., with Advent and Christmas) and with major feasts. What the Catholic liturgy has done in adapting the Bible to its religious festivals follows the way in which the Bible originally took its shape in the assemblies of ancient Israel.

In the light of this chapter how do we make the best use of our Bible as speaking God's inspired word. The following key suggestions unlock the door to the Bible as the word of GOD TODAY.

(1) The inspiration of the Bible reaches into our own lives and into our church. Our liturgical assemblies ought to combine the WORD of God with God's living presence among ourselves at prayer and instruction, in our contemporary world's efforts at social justice and moral wholesomeness. Thus the word of God becomes the living expression of GOD.

(2) The scriptures, as heard in our assemblies of prayer, enable us to become a living part, not only of our world today, but equally alive in the world of our ancestors, reaching back to Jesus and his disciples, to Ezra, Jeremiah, Joshua and Moses, to Abraham and Sarah. The Bible is a bond with the past, not so much by telling us the details of their lives as by infusing us with their courageous dedication and their onward thrust of hope. The blood which inspired them is our blood of life today.

(3) In reading the Bible with an eye to the past, we detect in ancient times the lively interchange of speakers and listeners, of questions and answers, of challenge and application. These ancient biblical assemblies impart vigor and bonding into our liturgy. If the details of the past are important, it is less for what they communicate about secular details or even religious names

and dates, than for how they involve us with our neighbor in church and in the needs of daily life.

(4) Scripture within the church evolves from the WORD of God to the word of GOD, if our liturgical ceremonies link the Bible with the profound hopes and sorrows of life today. A compassionate, living God is most present where life is most real in its agonies and possibilities. Liturgy and Bible enable us to discover this total presence of God.

Chapter Four

Traditions Alive

We have been approaching the Bible as we would a friend, loyal and caring, or as we would a counselor, wholesome and inspiring over the years. We have received and opened the Bible, and to our surprise we have discovered that this single book includes seventy-three books, forty-six in the Old Testament and twenty-seven in the New Testament!

In chapter one we unpacked some of these facts. We saw that the forty-six books in the Old Testament were arranged one after another carefully for theological reasons. In fact, the Jewish and Christian arrangements differ in order to accentuate their own unique message: the *Christian* way of indicating that history and prophecy point to the coming of the messiah, Jesus; the *Jewish* way of showing that faithful people center their lives around the Torah or five books of Moses and come regularly in pilgrimage to the Jerusalem temple. Chapter two focused upon two books, that of Exodus and Isaiah, impressing us with the concern of each editor to impart a religious message in the way that they put the material together. Each book of the Bible, therefore, has its own singular history, as its sermons and instructions were transmitted from a Moses or an Isaiah, to disciples, and from them to later generations, until an editor assembled the present book. Chapter three attempted to piece together the process by which an original event, like the flight of the Israelites out of Egypt, became the book of Exodus. We claim that liturgical celebrations at the major sanctuaries carry the major responsibility, not only for preserving the traditions but also for imparting the literary form of praise, prayer and instruction to them.

Our task in chapter four requires more careful reading of the biblical text than was necessary up till now. In the first three chapters we worked with the Bible *just as it is,* from one book to another, or within any single book from one chapter to another. Now we dig *into the text* to detect those earlier layers which lie between Moses or Isaiah, the originators of the traditions, and the final editing of their words and ministry into the five books of Moses and the prophecy of Isaiah. Disciples of Moses and Isaiah transmitted the masters' words and work in the sanctuaries and in other kinds of assemblies, until the editors of the books arranged these traditions according to their own special purpose.

As mentioned already, we *believe* (this word is used deliberately with a strong sense of faith) that from start to finish, from the original event or speaker, into sanctuary worship, to the final editor, *God was always present,* inspiring and directing, reaching a goal otherwise unattainable by the human authors. God takes ultimate responsibility for the Bible; it is the word of God. As similar as parts of the Bible are to other ancient near eastern literature, as forceful as may have been the intervention of people in the events or in the literary forms of the Bible, the Bible is different because of God's steady and continuous influence.

In fact, this divine impact, as mysterious as it was and continues to be, is the primary object of our search in the Bible. As mentioned in the introduction, we seek to shift the emphasis in Bible reading from the WORD of God to the word of GOD, from study to prayer, and from prayer to contemplative wonder in God's awesome presence. The wise man Sirach said it well. After concluding a major section of his book, he declared:

Although we speak much we cannot reach the end,
  and the sum of our words is: "God is all in all." . . .
When you praise the Lord, exalt him as much as you can;
  for God will surpass even that. . . .
Many things greater than these lie hidden,
  for we have seen but few of God's works (Sir 43:27–32).

We are viewing the Bible, not just as the word of God, but as the word of God in relation to a community of faith. Creative persons like Moses or Isaiah who responded to a serious crisis, disciples who remembered the earlier preaching, liturgical leaders who gathered the people for worship, editors who assembled the material into a single book, the community who came together in prayer to strengthen their hopes and receive comfort, all shared in God's inspiration of the Bible, each in its own unique way. The Bible is more the product of an *inspired tradition* than the work of an inspired writer.

We now look at the traditions behind the five books of Moses. Because we do not possess documents that reflect the early stages of the five books of Moses, our results are not always one hundred percent certain and the conclusions are continually being refined by scholars. Yet the *hypothesis* of earlier traditions answers most of the problems raised within these books as well as offers valuable insights into the religious message.

Four Major Traditions

Anyone who has seriously read the book of Genesis several times will have spotted doublets or even triplets, where an event or explanation is given more than once, with only slight differences. Working under the assumption that the editor was a reasonable person who acted always for a purpose, we ask ourselves why the similarities and why the differences.

At the beginning we notice two accounts of creation: Genesis 1:1–2:4a and 2:4b–3:24. Three times we meet the unhappy experience where the patriarch Abraham or Isaac presents his wife as only his sister, lest he be killed by a jealous admirer: Genesis 12:10–20; 20:1–18; 26:7–11. We honestly think that one time would have been more than enough. In the flood story we ferret out two timetables or sets of chronology, each of which makes sense but together they cause confusion. One is Genesis 7:4, 10, 12, 17; 8:6, 10, 12; the other, Genesis 7:6, 11, 24; 8:3b–5, 13a, 14. In the story of Joseph his eldest brother Reuben intervenes and the young man is sold to the Midianites, or we learn that it is Judah who intervenes and Joseph is sold to the Ishmaelites (Gen 37:12–36).

True, the same thing often happens more than once, especially for people who are compulsive. And who isn't? It is also true that the biblical style of reasoning is more circuitous and repetitive than ours.

Repetition, however, more easily happens when stories are passed down in singing and choral recitation. Even today we repeat key words or phrases, themes or melodies more often in singing or public speaking than we do in conversation or on the printed page. These facts, however, still do not account for the *differences* in style, vocabulary, and viewpoint, even in theological attitudes, which show up *repeatedly and consistently* within individual traditions.

Oral or public transmission, moreover, accounts for the way that one tradition eventually blends with another, for instance in the story of Noah's flood. The traditions were not put together into our present book of Genesis by scissors and paste as we would today, cutting one word or phrase or sentence from one printed document, another word or phrase or sentence from another printed document, and then pasting them together. When we sing or speak spontaneously, we mix phrases or words that occur from our memory. We slip from one story to another by a similarity of words or events.

Four traditions merged to form the five books of Moses. We call them the Yahwist, the Elohist, the Priestly and the Deuteronomist. The compenetration of these traditions, to form the five books of Moses, happened orally for the most part, sometimes unconsciously, most of the time with care and determination, particularly in the final editing.

Yahwist—The Entertainer

The originator of the Yahwist tradition may have been a minstrel, singing to people's delight at the royal court and also in the temple courtyard. In the preceding chapter we described the temple as a large open square surrounding a small shrine. The courtyard was open to everyone; the shrine was reserved to priests and nobility. The activity in the courtyard included prayers and sacrifice as well as instruction and entertainment, pleasant conversation and even sleep in a shady corner. Only the shrine was reserved exclusively for worship. The Yahwist must have gravitated away from the shrine toward the outer edges where pilgrims gathered as much for relaxation as for religious instruction.

The character of the Yahwist can be judged by reading its story of creation and the fall in Genesis 2:4b–3:24. The style is lively, colorful, conversational; a delicate psychological awareness pervades the account; unforgettable images are introduced; the events often lead to tragedy, yet the conclusion always turns around with new hope. The Yahwist was a loyal follower of the Davidic dynasty and loses no opportunity to enhance the tribe of Judah from which David sprang. Yet he was not above poking fun and satire at some of its foibles and sins. The Yahwist tended—like some interesting, holy people in each one's acquaintance—to be a slight bit irreverent, unafraid to introduce myths and stories because of a strong faith and devoted love at the base of it all.

While the first story of creation from the Priestly tradition (Gen 1:1–2:4a) follows a dignified, stately style with God always in full command, the Yahwist account of creation leaves us always in suspense (Gen 2:4b–3:24). The Lord God creates the earth and the heavens, but the earth is dry and barren. Humankind is created into a lonely existence. Animals are formed but these do not measure up for friendship and understanding. Humankind becomes man and woman, who are to cleave to one another as two in one body. The final words of chapter one, "naked and were not ashamed," already hint that their nakedness may lead to shame.

Chapter 3 of Genesis opens with obvious, mythological details. The story of the garden of paradise, lost by pride and sin, is told again, but with significant differences in Ezekiel 28:11–19, and again, but without sin, in Sirach 24. The story belonged to a common treasury of the ancient near east and was adapted to communicate religious truths. Every culture has its fairy tales, something similar to mythology, which entertain children but always have a serious punch for adults.

The Yahwist orchestrates a lively, insidious conversation between the serpent and the woman. The serpent first questions if God really commanded this, and the woman exaggerates by stat-

ing that God forbade them even to touch the fruit of the tree of
knowledge of good and evil. In Genesis 2:16–17 God said nothing about touching the fruit! Next God's motives are open to
suspicion, jealousy and fear. Once humankind has remade God to
its own image, rather than live obediently according to God's
image, it wants to act without God.

> So when the woman saw that the tree was good for food,
> and that it was a delight to the eyes, and that the tree was
> to be desired to make one wise, she took of its fruit and
> ate; and she also gave some to her husband, and he ate
> (Gen 3:6).

Exceptional insight into human psychology is apparent here.
The woman is cautious but is finally swayed by flattery and ambition; the man caves in without a struggle, just to be at peace with
the wife. Whatever our individual sexuality, each of us has the
woman and the man in our psychological makeup.

God seems to have lost control and must roam through the
garden and call out, "Where are you?" God is still searching for
us, gently calling our names, seriously inviting us to repentance
and renewal. We are still passing the blame, like Adam who
tells God:

> The woman whom thou gavest me to be with me, she
> gave me fruit of the tree, and I ate.

God is partly at fault because of "the woman whom *thou* gavest
me," but most of all blame is leveled on the woman who "gave
me fruit of the tree." Woman, when questioned by God, points to
the serpent as the culprit:

> The serpent beguiled me and I ate.

At least she has more integrity than the man and avoids the insinu-
ation that God shares the guilt.

The story ends upbeat. God first passes sentence upon serpent, woman and man. The serpent must hereafter crawl upon its belly. The woman shall long for a husband who will dominate her and for children who will be received through the pangs of birth. The man shall work by sweat in a land of thorns and thistles. Yet at the beginning of the sentencing, God announces to the serpent:

> I will put enmity between you and the woman,
> and between your seed and her seed;
> he shall bruise your head,
> and you shall bruise his heel (Gen 3:15).

The struggle and pain of sin continue into each new generation. While humankind is bruised in the heel, the serpent will eventually be completely crushed in the head. Sin brings sorrow, but sorrow and struggle can lead to atonement and victory.

Several literary or historical observations lead us further into the thought-patterns of the Yahwist. The Yahwist, we said, was a loyal subject of the Davidic crown, as we see in the important blessing given to David's ancestor Judah in Genesis 49:8–12. Yet he was also a charming, even cunning entertainer, with a keen sense of right and wrong. If he was singing this and other ballads at the royal court and for entertainment in the temple courtyard, could he have been thinking of David and Bathsheba in retelling the story of Adam and Eve? David, like Adam, began as an innocent youth (1 Sam 16:1–13; 17), was seduced by Bathsheba, the counterpart to Eve (2 Sam 11–12), and from this marriage came a family history of sorrow and bloodshed, as in Genesis 4 (2 Sam 13; 15; 18), yet also a promise of a blessing, as in Gen 3:15 (2 Sam 7) which finds fulfillment in Christ (Acts 2:20; Heb 1:5).

The Yahwist tradition, in its origins, drew upon world culture swirling around the court of David and Solomon. It reached deeply into the psyche of man and woman, of ruler and subject, to reveal hidden, shameful struggles between goodness and evil. These tendencies are universal and therefore reach back to the beginning. Original sin, in this account, was rooted more in the world conflict, swaying men and women beyond their power to control, placing them humbly before God who is the source of strength and wisdom. By incorporation into the family of faith, this "sin" is removed in that each person lives with the supports of faith, prayer and a community sense of God's presence.

The Yahwist, along with keen psychological insight and wide theological vision, manifests a flair for suspense and interlocking order. If we reread chapter three, we find that the sequence of introducing the three main actors is being continually reversed:

in sinning	*in interrogating*	*in sentencing*
serpent	man	serpent
woman	woman	woman
man	serpent	man

Woman seems to be the central figure. These and other details show the mark of a keen psychologist, a born entertainer, an expert singer of ballads, a master instructor in good and evil.

The Elohist—Prophet and Mystic

The Elohist tradition received its name from German scholars of the nineteenth century who recognized that it did not use the divine name Yahweh until this was revealed to Moses in chapter three of Exodus. The Yahwist tradition, on the contrary, calls God "Yahweh" already in chapter two of Genesis. Yahweh is generally translated LORD in most English Bibles, except the Jerusalem Bible, which maintains the Hebrew word. This divine name is never pronounced by orthodox Jews. It was used only once a year, on the feast of Atonement or Yom Kippur, when the high priest entered the holy of holies, the inner sanctum of the Jerusalem temple (Lev 16). In Orthodox synagogues today *adonai* or "Our Lord" substitutes for Yahweh; outside of the synagogue they simply say *ha-shem* or "the Name."

By way of a distraction, yet helpful in the range of Bible conversation, the word Jehovah resulted when people erroneously joined the consonants of Yahweh (can also be spelled Jahveh) with the vowels of *adonai*. In the latter case the initial "a" is very short, almost like a whispered "e," and the final "i" actually represents a consonant in the Hebrew language. The vowels, therefore, of *adonai* (the short "e," the "o" and the "a") were added to Hebrew manuscripts, starting around the seventh century A.D., because the word to be vocalized at this place was not Yahweh but *adonai*. Much later at the time of the Protestant reformation, when the Bible was being retranslated from Hebrew into various languages, vowels and consonants were read together as *Jehovah!*

The Elohist tradition circulated in the northern part of the land, the Yahwist in the south, especially at Jerusalem. The northern tribes were eventually deported by the Assyrians and lost to history. Whatever survived from the northern kingdom was brought south to Jerusalem. While the Elohist tradition is more deeply rooted in the Mosaic heritage and was a major source for the Yahwist tradition, it was eventually submerged within the Yahwist in the final editing of the five books of Moses.

The earliest mention of prophecy appears in the Elohist tradition: passages like Genesis 20:7, where Abraham is called a prophet; Numbers 11:24–30 where the seventy elders are gifted with prophecy and Moses exclaims: "Would that all the LORD's people were prophets, that the LORD would put his spirit upon them"; Numbers 12, where Moses is supreme among the prophets; Numbers 22–24, where the prophet Balaam predicts a glorious future for Israel. From the Elohist tradition we learn that prophecy was a major ingredient in leadership, a gift freely bestowed by God and not dependent upon class, rank or wealth.

The Elohist tradition shows itself more conscious of moral integrity. If we compare the three accounts where the patriarchs Abraham and Isaac, for fear of being murdered because of a beautiful wife, present Sarah or Rebekah as a sister, only the Elohist enters serious qualifications. In Genesis 20:1–18, God appears to the foreign king, warning him not to touch Sarah, for she is Abraham's wife. The Elohist explains that Abraham is not telling a lie, for Sarah is actually Abraham's half-sister. In the Yahwist accounts of Genesis 12:10–20 and 26:6–11 such caution is not manifest. It is not that one contradicts the other, only that one is more perceptive of moral expectations than the other. It is generally agreed that the Yahwist was more worldly than the Elohist, a fact which occasionally shows up in religious leadership today. While one is more spiritual with higher goals, the other is more sophisticated, more entertaining and more effective with certain groups of people.

While in the Yahwist tradition God walks in the garden of paradise, looking for Adam and Eve and calling out for them, in the Elohist tradition God is much more sublime, invisible and illusive. The Elohist speaks of God coming in a dream (Gen 20:5), in the midst of fire (Ex 3) and thunder (Ex 19). As mentioned already, the Elohist tradition tends to be submerged within the Yahwist, so that passages like Exodus 3 and 19 blend the two traditions together.

Chapter 3 of Exodus, even if the literary strands are sometimes difficult to disentangle, offers one of the most eloquent passages for Elohist spirituality. Sanctuary interest is apparent at once: Moses' father-in-law is called "the priest of Midian." Moses comes to "the mountain of God," possibly an ancient holy place, where "the angel of the Lord appeared to him in a flame of fire out of the midst of a bush." Mystified by the fire and sensing the presence of the divine, Moses turns aside to hear his name, "Moses! Moses!" God identifies himself:

I am the God of your ancestors, the God of Abraham, the God of Isaac, and the God of Jacob.

The Lord then said:

I have seen the affliction of my people who are in Egypt, and have heard their cry because of their taskmasters; I know their sufferings, and I have come down to deliver them out of the hand of the Egyptians and to bring them up out of that land to a good and broad land, a land flowing with milk and honey. . . . And now, behold, the cry of the people of Israel has come to me, and I have seen the oppression. . . . Come, I will send you to Pharaoh that you may bring forth my people, the children of Israel, out of Egypt.

When Moses asks to know the name of this God, God replied: "I am who I am." Moses is to say to the people:

> The LORD [Yahweh], the God of your ancestors, the God of Abraham, the God of Isaac, and the God of Jacob, has sent me to you.

Characteristic of prophecy and of biblical religion in its best moments is this sense of a personal, compassionate God. "I have seen their affliction." Prophecy vigorously defends the rights of the oppressed. This intuition comes clearly to the surface when God reveals himself to Moses atop Mount Sinai in one of the key, motivational passages in the book of Exodus (see chapter two of this book). While Moses holds the two tablets of the law in his arms, God passes by and declares:

> The LORD, the LORD, a God merciful and gracious, slow to anger, and abounding in steadfast love and faithfulness (Ex 34:6).

We are indebted to the Elohist for a revelation of God that becomes the most distinguishing feature of biblical religion, placing it head and shoulders over every other world religion.

The Priestly Legislator

The Yahwist tradition turns out to be the most entertaining and worldly, the least worried about stories with a touch of irreverence and mythology. The Elohist tradition leads us into a perception of God, close and compassionate in our human suffering, distant and sublime in our dreams and mystical prayer, prophetically demanding of moral integrity. The third tradition to be considered here, the Priestly, is the most stable. It undergirds the first four books of Moses, Genesis through Numbers; it is heavy with legislation and ritual prescriptions. The Yahwist is our fun person, the Elohist our mystic, the Priestly our steady support.

The Priestly documents moves with stately dignity, even if the language tends to be repetitious and abstract. It never regains its peak of literary grandeur in Genesis 1:1–2:4a, where an exalted rhythm flows in a series of refrains:

> And God said, let it be . . . and it was; And God saw that it was good, and after creating humankind male and female, God saw that it was very good; and it was evening and it was morning, the first . . . second . . . third day.

In this Priestly story of creation God remains majestic and transcendent, never, as in the Yahwist story, working with the mud of the earth to form a human being, nor walking in the garden looking and calling out for the couple. For the Priestly tradition God speaks and it is done. Typical of a tradition which contains most of Israel's laws for daily life and for the sanctuary, all depends upon the word and authority of God. If we were to read the Priestly tradition consecutively, linking the story of creation with the legislation, then we would catch the theological inference: if we obey, God's word will create a new paradise in our lives.

The Priestly tradition was the gridiron supporting the other traditions. The refrain, typical of the Priestly author, is repeated at key transitional moments in the first four books of Moses: "These are the generations of . . ." in Hebrew, *eleh toledoth.* The phrase completes the work of creation: "These are the generations of the heavens and the earth" (Gen 2:4a), and introduces the story of the descendants of Adam and Eve (Gen 5:1), of Noah (Gen 10:1), of Shem (Gen 11:10), of Terah the father of Abraham (Gen 11:27), of Isaac (Gen 25:19), of Jacob (Gen 37:2), of Moses and Aaron (Num 3:1).

The greater part of Israel's legislation, particularly in the books of Leviticus and Numbers, is attributed to this source which made its home at the Jerusalem temple.

The Deuteronomic Preacher

While the Priestly tradition represents the legal tradition of the *southern* Jerusalem temple, the Deuteronomic tradition contains the law code of the *northern* sanctuaries. Around the time of the collapse of the northern kingdom in 721 B.C., this tradition was carried south to Jerusalem. It may have influenced the reform of King Hezekiah (715–686 B.C.; 2 Kgs 18–20; 2 Chron 29–32). It was the book found in the renovation of the temple at the beginning of the reform of King Josiah (640–609 B.C.; 2 Kgs 22–23; 2 Chr 34–35). We are told:

> The high priest Hilkiah informed the scribe Shaphan, "I have found the book of the law in the temple of the LORD" (2 Kgs 22:8).

Josiah based his reform upon this document. At the same time the document was further strengthened and clarified, subject to new modifications and additions. The legislation about a single place of worship in chapter 12 of Deuteronomy was interpreted to mean Jerusalem alone. All other sanctuaries were demolished (2 Kgs 23:8–27). As happened in the Catholic Church at the Second Vatican Council, law codes and ritual books were revised and updated, places of worship were remodeled and simplified, and a new fervor spread throughout God's people.

By reading and comparing chapter 19 of Leviticus and chapters 14 and 15 of Deuteronomy, the differences between the Priestly and the Deuteronomic approach toward law show up at once. Leviticus, from the Priestly tradition, manifests a confident sense of authority; it repeats the refrain at the end of each law in chapter 19, "I am the LORD your God." By contrast, Deuteronomy shows a style of exhortation and an attitude of compassion. In chapter 14 it begins with this human touch in asking for obedience: "You are children of the LORD your God." Deuteronomy speaks of partaking of your food, even wine and strong drink, to make merry with your family before the Lord your God. And the kind admonition is added: "You shall not forsake the Levite who is within your towns, for he has no portion or inheritance with you" (v 27). Later the same care is to shown to "the sojourner, the fatherless, and the widow . . . that the LORD your God may bless you in all the work of your hands" (v 29).

The Deuteronomic touch of compassion reaches out to us, when we compare the two renditions of the ten commandments in the books of Moses. We refer especially to the commandment about keeping holy the sabbath day:

Elohist: Ex 20
Remember the sabbath day, to keep it holy . . . in it you shall not do any work, or your son, or your daughter, your manservant or the maidservant, or your cattle, or the sojourner . . . for in six days the LORD made heaven and earth, the sea, and all that is in them, and rested the seventh day; therefore the LORD blessed the seventh day and hallowed it.

Deuteronomist: Dt 5
Observe the sabbath day to keep it holy . . . in it you shall not do any work, you, or your son, or your daughter, your manservant or your maidservant, or your ox, or your ass, or any of your cattle, or the sojourner. . . . You were a servant in the land of Egypt and the LORD your God brought you out thence with a mighty hand and an outstretched arm; the LORD your God commanded you to keep the sabbath day.

The differences, minor though they be, are important. The separate readings are due to their transmission in sanctuary worship in the midst of sermons and exhortations. In Exodus 20 the Elohist tradition blends with the Priestly tradition and relies upon the authority and example of God who rested on the sabbath day. The Deuteronomic tradition seeks to win obedience from the motive of compassion and from the Israelites' memory of themselves once being slaves in Egypt. The Israelites are to share their compassion with foreigners in the land.

The Deuteronomic tradition was too massive in its content, too distinct in its style and spirituality, to be integrated into the other three traditions. The book of Deuteronomy remained separate at the end. As a result, the Priestly document was used as the basis and underpinning of the first four books; the Elohist and especially the Yahwist were incorporated into it. This work constituted Genesis, Exodus, Leviticus and Numbers. The spirit of Moses, accordingly, survived in two principal documents, each with its specific attitudes and emphases. Likewise, in the New Testament the spirit of Jesus continues in four gospels.

Conclusion

As great as Moses was, he was limited by time and space. As inspired as he was as revealer of God's will and as God's instrument for saving the Israelites, nonetheless Moses' words and work had to be adapted to the needs and problems of later generations. Moses died on the eastern side of the river Jordan and his aide Joshua was to complete the mission of Moses (Dt 34). Moses' mantle fell upon the shoulders of new leaders, new lawmakers, new prophets. This transfer of authority is symbolized in the fact that while Moses alone ascends Mount Sinai in chapter 19 of Exodus to receive the covenant and laws, others accompany Moses in chapter 24 when the law and covenant are sealed in a ritual of blood that was to continue in the sanctuaries of Israel.

Four major groups of disciples continued with the inspiration of Moses. Two of these, the Yahwist and the Elohist, were mostly concerned with stories; two others, the Priestly and the Deuteronomic, with legislation. Each tradition, with its own disciples, was instructing Israelites how to live according to the spirit of Moses. Today we are as much influenced and guided by the lives of saintly people as we are by rules and regulations, perhaps more by our saints than by our legislators. Good example spreads its influence the farthest.

The Yahwist and Elohist traditions frequently parallel each other with stories about the first generations of Israelites. The Elohist account circulated in the sanctuaries of the north, the Yahwist in the south. The Yahwist highlighted entertainment as much as edification. When the northern kingdom collapsed, the Elohist stories were brought to Jerusalem and gradually merged with the Yahwist. Both of these traditions were incorporated into the Priestly, as examples of holy people in keeping the law. This merger produced the books of Genesis, Exodus, Leviticus and Numbers. The northern law book remained separate as the book of Deuteronomy.

It was mentioned already that the synagogue reading of the last chapter of Deuteronomy never ends at that point. Immediately the lector starts over again with chapter one of Genesis. For Israelites the study of the law was never to end. There was continuous need of adapting it, so that the spirit of Moses remained alive and was never confined to dead letters. This vitality, in touch with each new age, was easier in those days than in ours. Israelites depended upon the *oral* transmission in an *assembly,* with explanation and application. An example of this was seen in the preceding chapter of this book in our study of the assembly of Ezra (Neh 8:1–8). We tend to be too dependent upon *written* words and our *individual* study of them. Our modern setting restricts and privatizes our appreciation of the Bible.

Once again, we see in ancient biblical times an example of how the Catholic Church continuously presents the Bible. We hold that the Bible is to be interpreted within the tradition of the church. We adapt the reading of the Bible to our liturgical year and to the clarification of doctrine. This approach to the Bible was summarized in the document on Revelation from Vatican II. The council stressed, first: "holy scripture must be read and interpreted according to the same Spirit by whom it was written"; second, "the living tradition of the whole church must be taken into account." Through this interaction of scripture and tradition, "the judgment of the church may mature."

The council document brings together the two sides of the question. Through scripture the judgment of the church matures, and through the church the correct meaning and application of scripture are achieved. Scripture lives as new questions and solutions are discussed in modern times by the church. As the church is guided by its treasury of tradition and its pastoral concerns, scripture reaches its correct meaning in any age.

The work of Moses within various traditions, united in the bonds of the one Bible, proclaimed and applied through worship and preaching, begins over and over again, as the church, in the steps of its Jewish ancestors, passes from the final chapter of Deuteronomy to the opening chapter of Genesis about creation. Together we await the creation of the new heavens and the new earth, as we listen obediently to the word of God (Is 65:17–25; Rev 21:1–4).

This chapter in our study of the Old Testament introduces us to new ways in transforming the WORD of God into the word of GOD, this time by alerting us to the rich variety of traditions in the Bible. No single human expression, though inspired by the Holy Spirit and communicated in the family of God's saintly people, exhausts the richness of God's truth and compassion; each tradition hints to a mystery beyond its horizon.

(1) In opening our Bible for prayer and study, we first attend, as mentioned in earlier chapters of this book, to the sequence of the many books and to the order of material within any single book. Everything is so arranged that a message is communicated to us about God and God's hopes for us. We realize that this material originated with saintly individuals, whose disciples remembered and transmitted the message of their teacher, particularly within sanctuary worship. Here worship added its strong need of exhortation and praise, instruction and ritual.

(2) The fourth chapter of our study focused upon earlier pre-biblical stages, before the Bible became the book now in our hands. By reading and rereading the Bible we begin to detect similarities and differences, and we ask: Why? The WORD of God turns into the Word of GOD as we perceive that the differences and similarities locate the many localities and personalities where God is present to inspire and instruct us. The word is not restricted to storytellers nor to mystics, not to legislators nor to prophets. The differences do not lead to contradictions and error. Rather we delight in the variety of God's presence. We are consoled, even in our idiosyncrasies, that each of us bears a unique image of God, so rich and so overwhelming as to defy every human limitation. The WORD of God in its differences shifts the emphasis to the word of GOD—a God even beyond the limits of the sacred words of the Bible.

(3) Yet, this word with all its diversity does not come to us scattered in many places without any attempt at stitching to-

gether. The many books of the Bible (as we saw to be the original meaning of Bible or *biblia* in the Greek language) are united in our single Bible; the many traditions about Moses were united in the five books which become in Jewish tradition the single Torah. The various sanctuaries of Israel were eventually blended into the worship of the single Jerusalem temple. After we have spotted the various traditions, we need to unite them again, cast the colors and images of one upon the other, so that we are led in adoration before the one God of Israel:

> Hear, O Israel: The LORD our God is one LORD; and you shall love the LORD your God with all your heart, and with all your soul, and with all your might (Dt 6:4–5).

Chapter Five

The Historical Reality Behind the Bible

In opening our Bible we have before us a *religious document,* based on historical data, but *not a history book.* The opposite seems true, however, when we turn to the table of contents for the Old Testament in the New American Bible and the New Jerusalem Bible. Our eyes fall upon a section entitled "Historical Books." We naturally ask: Does the Old Testament at least partially consist of historical books?

This question was already discussed in chapter one, where we saw that the title "historical books" did not mean history as it is written today, but rather a theological perception that each event was leading up to "the fullness of time," the messianic era, inaugurated by Jesus Christ (Eph 1:10). In the same chapter we saw that the Jewish division, which was accepted in the New Testament (Lk 24:44), had no section called "Historical Books," but rather located most of these books under the title of prophecy. The books of Samuel and Kings, for instance, were considered a prophetical judgment upon the fidelity of Israel to its covenant and to its God of compassion and justice.

Chapter two explained how history entered into the biblical books. Very often the original event, like the flight from Egypt, as real as it was for Israel, never would have made history. It had no impact upon any other nation and probably would have been forgotten by Israel, except for two reasons. First, God would not give up on this chosen people and allow them to die in the desert wilderness of Sinai; second, Israel began to commemorate the flight to freedom in liturgical ceremonies which drew ever larger numbers of people into the meaning of that event. Understood in this context, liturgy made history, for it implanted the earlier event firmly within the consciousness of Israel and continued its influence in the lives of ongoing generations of Israelites.

How Much Is Historical?

If even the "historical books" of the Old Testament are a blend of the original event with later liturgical explanations and celebrations, we ask: How much of the material in these books is history and how much is not, and how do we tell the difference?

We answer these questions by turning to a key example, the exodus out of Egypt and the wandering in the Sinai wilderness under the direction of Moses. The exodus became the model for faith in God as liberator from sin and oppression. As the exodus was celebrated in the liturgy, the original, seemingly insignificant event was transformed into one of prime importance for Israel. From the exodus tradition, the chosen people were able to muster the faith to believe in God when they were faced with mammoth problems, and afterward they had the language to praise God as their liberator and savior.

Biblical traditions included the original event as well as its reliving and its retelling in times of worship. History, therefore, included a long inspired tradition, in which Israel experienced over and over again the great redemptive moments of the past, and in so doing retold the event with contemporary language and imagery. The Bible, accordingly, included much more history than we give it credit for. In the case of the exodus, not only was the liberation under Moses' leadership proclaimed, but other, later acts of God in Israel's history.

Biblical books gradually took shape from the songs, creeds and narratives prominent in sanctuary worship, from the preaching of the prophets and from palace archives. Temple personnel provided the scribes who were responsible for the final gathering into our biblical books. It is not easy to reconstruct the history behind this complex development.

An example from church documents may exemplify our

problem. The task of writing the history of Christianity would become all the more formidable than what it is if we had to depend exclusively on liturgical books from post Vatican II days like the Lectionary and the Sacramentary for Sunday and weekday masses, on summaries of the great councils of the church, and other secular documents which refer to Christianity only incidentally and rarely at that.

Another example comes from the family background of most Americans. Our ancestors undertook an exodus from other countries. The fact is beyond dispute, but how many of us can write a diary, year by year, of our family history over the past two hundred years? How many know the name of the ship which brought our ancestors to the shores of the United States? How many can retrace the paths taken by their grandparents on their difficult way from Central and South America. As a thumbnail rule, the Bible generally offers the *fact* of the first event but submerges the fact in later applications and celebrations. If this situation makes it difficult for us to deal with a modern skeptic, then we recall once again that the Bible, like the Sacramentary and Lectionary for the Eucharist, *was not composed for skeptics but for believers,* women and men who wanted to celebrate God's great redemptive deeds of former ages in their own contemporary families and communities.

A Unique Kind of History and Theology

Scholars often speak of finding a special kind of history in the Bible, called "salvation history." Yet salvation is basically a mystery of faith which cannot be proven in human ways nor adequately described in human history. Even if we possessed secular documents to establish that Moses led the Israelite people out of Egypt and that Jesus died on the cross, this data would never prove that God was acting through Moses and that Jesus' death won the salvation of the world. If we cannot prove salvation from historical documents, can we properly speak of salvation history? If the history is submerged within documents of faith, then the Bible is a unique kind of history.

On the other hand, the Bible is not a *theoretical* treatise on a religious subject; it does not have separate chapters on the existence and nature of God, nor on the vocation of marriage and ministry. The Bible is theology rooted in the sequence of human events as retold within liturgical celebrations. Many human events entered into the Bible, often with a major impact on Israelite theology. The surrounding Gentile nations, for instance, contributed to the architecture of the Israelite temple and much later to its destruction. The role of kings in the ancient near east helped to form Israel's image of the promised messiah. The gospel of Luke carefully links the coming of Jesus as savior with major historical figures and events in Palestine and in the Roman empire (Lk 1:5; 2:1–5; 3:1–2, 23–38).

Biblical theology is distinguished from other methods of organizing doctrine and morals in the way that religious ideas *develop* from one age to another, and, as mentioned already, from the way that *crucial historical moments,* like the Babylonian destruction of Jerusalem, affected the advance of theology in Israel. We may not be able to cross all the t's and dot all the i's in spelling out the history of Israel, but the large historical background is securely in place, and the influence of world events upon Israel's understanding of God and God's expectations is clear. We now investigate some of this interaction of history and theology in the Old Testament.

Preparing for the Mosaic Covenant: 1850–1550 B.C.

The book of Genesis sees Israel's *origin,* as the word "Genesis" means, first within a universal panorama of the heavens and the earth and of humankind spread across the surface of the earth (chapters 1–11) and then within the geography and events of the near east (chapters 12–50).

Theologically the Bible is declaring that Israel cannot reach its goal as intended by God, isolated like an orphan from the rest of the members of its family. The book of Genesis insists that God has created one human family with a single home, the planet earth, and a single history whose lines must eventually join together. Chapter 11 of Genesis may not divide the human race according to modern racial and ethnic groups, but theologically it is declaring that God was planning for Abraham and Sarah, the parents of Israel, to emerge within the family of nations in the ancient middle east.

The journey of Abraham and Sarah from Ur of the Chaldees, in the south of modern Iraq, northeast to Haran in modern Syria, and eventually southeast to Palestine corresponds with the line of political upheavals in the second millennium. Streams of Asiatics were on the move, pouring south into Egypt. Many of the former city states in Palestine have been abandoned, and the country is again open to new settlers and their herds of livestock. Eventually these Asiatics took control of Egypt and established the fifteenth and sixteenth dynasties of that land. These facts explain how Joseph, an Asiatic, rose to power as chief minister of the land and why the family of Jacob migrated into Egypt. Here the book of Genesis ends.

Several significant theological conclusions can be drawn from the historical data in Genesis 12–50. We see that the patriarchs and their families did not establish a new religion.

The patriarchs accepted many aspects of local religions. Abraham and Sarah stopped at places which archaeology has identified as traditional shrines: Shechem, Bethel and Beer-sheba. From a people called Canaanites they learned their language and alphabet, their methods of grazing cattle and farming, their architecture for homes and shrines, in fact their entire culture and way of living. They used the Canaanite name, *el,* for their God.

In Egypt the patriarchs encountered one of the highest civilizations known in ancient times. The great pyramids (on the western edge of modern Cairo) were already six hundred years old! Egyptian health care reached a peak never attained throughout the entire Old Testament.

Theologically we conclude that God did not reveal culture and its achievements, political organization and leadership, the external format for religion like temple architecture, ritual and leadership. History contributed this background to the religious account of the Bible.

As dependent as the Bible is upon its historical setting, however, the Bible turns out differently from the religion of other ancient peoples. Israel's religion basically does not depend upon race or nationality, nor upon power and prestige, nor again upon culture and politics. Israel's religion is due to God's compassion and care for homeless people and God's intervention in their regard.

In the Bible religion springs from *compassion,* a virtue deeply rooted in human nature. Yet from human experience it is the virtue most difficult to sustain over the long haul. God not only brought this virtue from its depth to the outer surface of living but heightened in a supernatural way Israel's sense of its presence.

The Mosaic Covenant: ca. 1250 B.C.

This forty to fifty year period is the most important theologically for the Old Testament; it is likewise the most elusive historically. Because the Israelites are alone in the Sinai wilderness, with little or no contact with the surrounding nations, we cannot draw upon other outside sources to reconstruct life. And the Bible itself is too sketchy for us confidently to write the history of the wilderness period. As an example, a very similar episode happens twice in different places, but the name of the place is the same (Ex 17:1–7; Num 20:1–13).

Still another, more internal reason blurs this time of Israel's existence. Sinai never acquired the status of a sanctuary in Israel's religion. Its memories were preserved, first of all at Gilgal, a sanctuary on the western shore of the river Jordan, just north of the Dead Sea, and then at Jerusalem. Psalm 114 combines the passage through the Red Sea with that through the river Jordan:

When Israel went forth from Egypt,
    the house of Jacob from a people of strange language,
Judah became the LORD's sanctuary,
    Israel his dominion.
The sea looked and fled,
    Jordan turned back.
The mountains skipped like rams,
    the hills like lambs.

There are no mountains near the Red Sea, so the scenario of Psalm 114 comes from the southern part of the river Jordan and the sanctuary at Gilgal. The *fact* of the journey through the Red Sea is submerged within the *geographical setting and liturgical ceremonies* at the sanctuary of Gilgal.

Still another ancient poem, Psalm 68, moves away from the Sinai wilderness to center festivities at Jerusalem's temple. The psalm opens with the call to break camp in the wilderness from Num 10:35:

> Let God arise, let his enemies be scattered;
>   let those who hate him flee before him!

The text of Psalm 68 moves forward majestically, drawing upon models of the finest Canaanite poetry, with Sinai quaking at the presence of God (v 8). It recalls the victories of the judges (vv 11–14), and then, reaching Jerusalem, it rehearses a triumphal procession, beginning with:

> Why look you with envy, O many-peaked mountain,
>   at the mount which God desired for his abode,
>   yea, where the LORD will dwell for ever (v 16)?

Geographically Sinai was left behind; theologically its traditions were reexperienced at the Jerusalem temple.

The site of Mount Sinai is still argued. The Bible uses various names: "Horeb" according to northern traditions of the Bible like Deuteronomy and 1 Kings; "Sinai" according to southern traditions; or sometimes very simply the "mountain of God." St. Jerome, the foremost biblical scholar of the fourth to fifth century, located it at Serabit el-Khadim to the northwest, still other authorities in northern Arabia. Jebel Musa or Mount Moses, the local name for Mount Sinai, is defended by most archaeologists, including Roland de Vaux, O.P.

We have already discussed in chapter two the central theological importance of the revelation to Moses during this formative period of Israel's existence. That so little remains for historical verification points out the precise nature of the Bible as primarily a religious document to be accepted on faith and to be relived in each new age of Israel or the church.

It is historically unreasonable to deny Israel this piece of its history, so forceful has it remained in the chosen people's memory. It is also historically impossible to *prove* most details of the wilderness experience. If history is an *exact, documented* science about events with strong impact beyond themselves, then very little history exists in Exodus through Deuteronomy. Yet these books are firmly fixed in real events which became the substance of Israel's liturgy for centuries thereafter.

Covenantal Religion: 1200–587 B.C.

These years span the period between Israel's entrance into the promised land at the river Jordan to the appearance of the classical prophets, those with books to their name.

Further evidence has come forth over the last thirty years from archaeology and sociology, sciences concerned with digging up ancient sites and reconstructing the social setting, to determine what happened during the Israelite settlement of the land. Many scholars are convinced that the Israelites upon entering the land did not slaughter its inhabitants, an impression left with us by the book of Joshua. If we keep reading from the next book, that of Judges, we find many Canaanites still in the land.

Documents like the Tell Amarna tablets from Egypt inform us that the land was seething with unrest and revolt. Slaves were breaking away. Mercenary troops were deserting the petty kings, and some of these kings were separating themselves from Egypt. Generals of military forces were looking for ways to advance themselves. The Israelites were still another group of people seeking freedom and dignity. They made treaties with local groups, like those at Shechem (Jos 8:30–35) and others at Gibeon (Jos 9:3–10:15). They fought when forced into battle. Israel provided the leadership of a large, liberation movement, rallying many people around the religious banner of the Mosaic covenant.

The form of government favored local independence for individual tribes. Several times a year they gathered at important shrines like Gilgal, Shiloh, Dan and Bethel to renew their bond of union in the worship of the same God and in the expectations of the covenant (Jos 24). Yet this fragile political unity was not enough to withstand the threat of the Philistines, a sea people who had invaded Palestine from the Mediterranean.

To offset this threat, the tribes of Israel united under the monarchy of David. The two books of Samuel narrate this development. Such a radical innovation as kingship was due to the intervention of prophetic figures like Samuel (1 Sam 8–11; 16). Yet as we move through the two books of Kings, we are appalled at the many excesses of royal authority. The editor of this vast material subjected the monarchy to a severe judgment, with dethronement, the destruction of the capital city, Jerusalem, and the exile of the people in 587 B.C. Much of this period can be fleshed out from documents obtained from the archives of Assyria and Babylon.

Theologically, the kingdom of David and Solomon left a memory of what God wants: a kingdom uniting Israel peacefully with other nations; a king who would be God's favored one, indeed bearing the title "Son of God" (Pss 2; 110). Despite the destruction of the kingdom this hope remained, as in the psalms and in the two books of Chronicles, only now it is invested in a new king to be raised up, mysteriously, by God in the future. We call this hope "messianic."

Prophetic Challenge: 760–587 B.C.

Prophecy first appeared in centers at Bethel, Ramah, Gibeath-Elohim and Gilgal (1 Sam 9–10; 2 Kgs 2) or with individuals like Elijah and Elisha (1 Kgs 17–2 Kgs 13). While these prophets cared for the poor and defended helpless people (1 Kgs 21), nonetheless serious signs of greed, jealousy and ambition began to show up in their midst (1 Kgs 22; Mic 3).

Another group of religious reformers emerged, so outraged by these degenerate prophets (Jer 28) that they disassociated themselves even from the title of prophet. Amos reacted angrily when called a prophet or seer:

> I am no prophet, nor a prophet's son; but I am a herds-
> man, and a dresser of sycamore trees, and the LORD took
> me from following the flock, and the LORD said to me,
> "Go, prophesy to my people Israel" (7:14–15).

While Amos follows God's inspiration in prophesying, he does
not tolerate the title of prophet and repudiates what it stands for.

Though denying all association with prophecy, Amos was the
first in a series of religious leaders who come to mind at once
when the word "prophet" enters a discussion. For this reason
scholars call them the "classical prophets." They are those with
books to their name. For this reason they were once called "writing prophets," yet this title has receded from use. The classical
prophets were primarily preachers of the word, not writers at a
desk. Frequently it was their disciples who gradually put their
preaching into written form (cf. Jer 36).

Eloquent preachers that they were, the classical prophets
responded to immediate hopes and addressed the problems at
hand. All of them, however, eventually saw no hope except
through the purifying fires of destruction and exile. Theology
thus reached beyond the boundaries of history.

Historically we can learn more from these prophets about the
political and social environment of Israelite life than from any
other biblical source. If the prophetical books turn out to be
difficult for us to read, because of their allusions to kings,
treaties and foreign nations, to social abuses, to places like "the
highway to the Fuller's Field" (Is 7:3), these same details made
the message all the more *evident to their listeners.* The people
understood the prophets so well that they hounded, abused and
drove them out. The prophecy of Jeremiah is our best source for
this hostile reaction (cf. Jer 26). His message was all too plain.

The Cauldron of the Exile: 587–539 B.C.

Israel thought of itself as forgotten by Yahweh and scattered
to the ends of the earth. Its desperation bordered on despair, as
we listen to the mournful dirges in the book of Lamentations:

Jerusalem remembers
in the days of her affliction and bitterness
all the precious things
that were hers from days of old.
When her people fell into the hands of the foe,
and there was none to help her,
the foe gloated over her,
mocking at her downfall (Lam 1:7).

In the frigid darkness of this arctic winter two voices warmed the hearts of the people. One of these, Ezekiel, endeavored to revive the people's hope along the lines once dominant at the Jerusalem temple. In chapters 40–48 Ezekiel reorganizes the people around the temple. From its altar life-giving water will flow to change even the Dead Sea into fresh water (Ez 47:1–12). The prophet is speaking symbolically, and according to this metaphor life depends upon temple ritual and is restricted to the land of Israel.

Somewhat later another prophet was called to comfort the exiles. Without a name, with his prophecy attached to the preaching of the great Isaiah of Jerusalem, he is generally called "Second Isaiah." His rhapsodic poetry is found in Isaiah 40–55. (See chapter two of this book for a study of the prophecy of Isaiah.) His gaze reached to the ends of the earth from whence he calls, not only those Israelites who have apostasized and gone over into the ranks of the Babylonians, but foreigners as well to participate in the covenant:

And now the LORD says,
who formed me from the womb to be his servant,
to bring Jacob back to him,
and that Israel might be gathered to him . . . .
The LORD says,
"It is too light a thing that you should be my servant
to raise up the tribes of Jacob
and to restore the preserved of Israel;
I will give you as a light to the nations, that my salvation
may reach to the end of the earth" (Is 49:5–6).

Out of the desperation of the exile there arose a faith that Yahweh will not only create a new Israel but will transform the universe for the sake of this chosen people.

Restoration and the Long Wait: After 539 B.C.

Strange as it may seem, no period of Israelite history, except for the Mosaic age, is more difficult to reconstruct than the final five hundred years before the coming of Christ, especially those years covered by Old Testament books. The clouds open and light shines only on three periods:

537–500, immediately after the return from exile;
445–428, during the reform of Nehemiah and Ezra;
167–143, during the Maccabean revolt.

Immediately after the return from exile the prophecies of Haggai, Zechariah (chapters 1–8), and Joel show how Israel regrouped, rejected foreigners and settled into "a day of small things" (Zech 4:10). The author of 1–2 Chronicles sets out at this time to rewrite 1–2 Samuel and 1–2 Kings, in order to center the earlier history more exclusively around the temple. The other period, between 445 and 428 B.C., is illumined by the prophecy of Malachi as well as by the books of Ezra and Nehemiah. The problems are sternly and effectively addressed by Ezra, as we saw already in chapter three of this book.

Israel became a theocracy, a small enclave centering round the Jerusalem temple, overlooked by world history, happy enough to be left alone. Alexander the Great marched up and down the coast, to be ignored by the Bible. Only when persecution strikes does Jerusalem reenter history through the two books of Maccabees (167–143 B.C.). Jerusalem again lapses into darkness, historically speaking, until the Romans appear on the scene in 63 B.C. The light of history is too weak for us to be absolutely certain about the Jews who settled along the Dead Sea, eventually to produce what we know as the Dead Sea Scrolls.

While the attitude in and around Jerusalem was hostile to

outsiders, other biblical books looked more favorably toward the nations, as we see in Isaiah 56–66, Jonah and Tobit. The Jews living in Egypt attempted to translate their holy scriptures in a way more understandable in their Greek culture. This Greek Bible, called the Septuagint, was the one with extra books (see chapter one), adopted by Christians.

While some Jews returned to Palestine after the exile, most remained scattered in Egypt and across the northern coast of Africa, in Lebanon and Syria, stretching into Greece and beyond to Rome and even Spain. The more fervent came on pilgrimage to Jerusalem. Most remained Jews, but some were more open to Gentile ways. It was to these Jews of the diaspora, as they came to be called ("diaspora" means, in Greek, to scatter), that Paul and the apostles first went to preach the messiah Jesus.

Conclusion

As we open our Bible and ask what is historical or not, the following norms may keep us from seeking too much history and too little theology and from presuming that the theology's reliability depends upon the Bible's credentials as primarily an historical document.

1. The details of Israel's history are securely established only when Israel possessed its own political identity and was in close contact with other nations. For this reason the period of the kingdom from David up till the exile (1004–539 B.C.) turns out to be the clearest. The most crucial period in the formation of Israel, that of Moses, remains one of the most obscure, for here we depend only on the Bible. Because the purpose of the Bible was not to reconstruct past events but to enable future generations to live the covenant within their own contemporary hopes and problems, even a period as crucial to biblical religion as that of Moses remains wrapped in darkness, historically speaking. When Israel became a theocracy in the post-exilic period, again we benefit from theological insights, but we have little historical data available to us.

It is unjustifiable to deny reality to the patriarchal and Mosaic periods because there is little historical data affirmed by outside documentation. No respectable scholar doubts the reality of the last five hundred years of the Old Testament, the period before Christ, even though its historical credentials are weak. At the same time it is wise to concentrate on religious questions, not on historical details, when discussing the age of the patriarchs or of Moses or the half-century before Christ. This advice is most applicable when reading the first eleven chapters of Genesis. This period is known as pre-history, a term that actually denies history, for it deals with a long stretch of time when we have no human documentation, only vague evidence of human habitation.

2. What is clear throughout the Bible is that God is a savior, intervening in space and time, within the real lives of people. The Bible everywhere presumes that its text is a theological reflection upon what was really happening. As a *religious* document of God's action in the life and times of Israel, individual traditions will be frequently updated to meet new challenges and hopes. As a result, one religious interpretation is inserted into another and the various historical periods are meshed together. In this sense the Bible has so much reality that the history becomes obscure in the many layers that merge in the text.

3. As we saw in the preceding chapter of this book, the Bible is primarily a book for worship and prayer. It does not depend upon any specific historical circumstance in the life of its believers. It can be applied to any class of people anywhere, anytime. But it must be applied, and that means we stand in need of religious leaders who academically know their Bible and pastorally know their people. Then the Bible will continue to impact secular history through the strength of people's faith and their worship together of a compassionate God.

Chapter Six

Awaiting the Messiah

Most Christians turn to the Old Testament to know more about Jesus, the promised messiah and savior of the world. Up till now, however, this aspect of the Old Testament has seldom, and then only indirectly, entered into our discussion. Yet we have never been orphans separated from our Christian home, at least not for long! We have been turning to the Bible as Jesus would have done—without the New Testament! The Bible for Jesus was a collection of sacred traditions, received from his Jewish ancestry, for temple and synagogue services as well as for instruction and personal prayer. Through long meditation upon this sacred heritage of his ancestors, Jesus was able to say to the disciples on the night of the resurrection:

> "Everything written about me in the law of Moses and the prophets and the psalms must be fulfilled." Then he opened their minds to understand the scriptures, and said to them, "Thus it is written" (Lk 24:44–45).

Because we too have reflected upon the law, the prophets and the writings through the previous five chapters of this book, we rightly want to know how these holy scriptures found their fulfillment in Jesus.

Jesus never turned to the holy scriptures for history and geography but rather for a religious insight into the meaning of life and mission. We too have seen that the Bible never remained simply an eye-witness account of exactly what happened once upon a time. Biblical traditions were carefully but repeatedly revised and adapted, especially at times of crisis or renewal. New generations would then appreciate, first God's grace-filled, saving presence in their lives, and second a bond of continuity with the faith of their ancestors. What God did then, God continued to do in the new and different circumstances of a later age. The Bible, in other words, is a blend of God's ancient activity with God's contemporary presence.

The most important task of our faith in working with the Bible is to allow the WORD of God to become the word of GOD, a subtle but most important shift of emphasis. God is always alive, never buried in the past (Ps 42:2), as the divine name Yahweh implies: "The one who is [always there with you]" (Ex 3:11–17). Just as the living God was always inspiring the people to move beyond the past and to update its ancient traditions, the same God of incomprehensible wonder could not be exhausted by what happened in the present moment.

The present never lived up to God's hopes and so was being continually oriented toward the future. To this extent the Old Testament is messianic in every line. Every word which came from God released such insights into God's mysterious life and into God's ideals for the chosen people that each syllable of the word seemed to reach beyond the present into the unknown future. The WORD of God possessed an inner dynamism to be transferred into the word of GOD. The *word* which can be rationally investigated for its historical and literary data modulates into the wondrous, even at times ecstatic presence of *God*.

Yet awaiting the messiah means more than being hopeful and optimistic about the future, more than being ecstatic at prayer. We now search what the letter to the Hebrews described as the "many and various ways God spoke of old to our ancestors" about Jesus (Heb 1:1).

Future Orientation in the Present Moment

The attitude of awaiting the messiah developed gradually. After the children of Israel had been delivered from Egyptian oppression and led into the promised land, they were so enthusiastic in thanking God for the joy of the present moment that little or no energy or need was at hand for thinking about the future. The same spirit of gratitude sings in our own hearts at great moments like a wedding or the birth of a child, an ordination to the priesthood or a profession of religious vows, a new employment or even our graduation from school. In our joy we would be satisfied if the world stopped!

The harvest festival was one of these moments for Israel. After professing their "creed" of what God has done through Abraham, Moses and Joshua (see chapter three), they confess that their present joy is a continuation of these great acts of God:

> The LORD has brought *us* out of Egypt with a mighty hand an outstretched arm, with great terror, with signs and wonders; and he brought *us* into this land, a land flowing with milk and honey. And behold, now *I* bring the first of the fruit of the ground, which thou, O LORD, hast given *me* (Dt 26:8–10).

They are then told:

> You shall rejoice in all the good which the LORD your God has given to you and to your house, you, and the Levite, and the sojourner who is among you (Dt 26:11).

This sense of "now," "this day," "we," "ourselves," "you," and "your house" pervades the book of Deuteronomy (cf. Dt 5:1–5). The past continued to be alive in the contemporary moment.

The past, moreover, was liberated of many of its problems and dark days and lived more gloriously in the present moment than ever in the past. In another book, whose spirit and theology were formed through the traditions of Deuteronomy, Joshua declares:

> And now, I am about to go the way of all the earth, and you know in your hearts and souls, all of you, that not one thing has failed of all the good things which the

LORD your God promised concerning you; all have come
to pass for you, not one of them has failed (Jos 23:14).

If we stopped here, we may as well close the Bible and forget
about awaiting the messiah. Yet the very next sentence issues a
warning and instruction for the future:

Just as all the good things which the LORD your God had
promised concerning you have been fulfilled for you, so
the LORD will bring upon you all the evil things, until he
has destroyed you from off this good land which the
LORD your God has given you, if you transgress the covenant of the LORD your God (Jos 23:15–16).

Excitement over the present moment, therefore, never cancelled
out a future orientation. At least a hint of messianic hopes always
stirred in people's bones.

It has been mentioned already that the Israelites never exhausted the message and promises of the Torah or the five books
of Moses. Once they had come to the end of it (Dt 34:12), the
lector immediately began reading from chapter 1 of Genesis. In
Deuteronomy 34 Moses, the perfect model of God's servant,
against whom every other Israelite is to be measured and judged,
died overlooking the promised land. No matter how long the
Israelites lived in the land, they were always with Moses on the
eastern bank of the Jordan, waiting to cross and take possession of
the promises. Out of this attitude developed their hopes for the
future, so that Israel took up the posture of awaiting the Messiah.

The Hebrew Word "Messiah"

Before investigating this hope, we note that "messiah" trans-
literates a Hebrew word which means "the anointed one." Translated into Greek, it became "christos," one of the most important
titles for Jesus of Nazareth. "Messiah" originally referred to the
king, anointed with sacred oil at the time of the coronation (1
Sam 10:1; 16:13; Ps 2:2). Later, when royalty disappeared and its

role was taken over by the high priest, the ceremony of anointing with oil became part of the high priest's investiture (Zech 4:14; 6:11), at which time the new ritual was incorporated into the law book of Moses (Lev 8).

At times we use the word "messianic" in a broad, really imprecise sense, not of an anointed king or priest but of any person or group or even a statement representing Israel's hopes for renewal.

All this may seem confusing—and it is! Yet it is no more perplexing than Christian expectations for the second coming of Jesus and for the rewards after death. Even St. Paul seems to have expected an imminent return of Jesus in his first letter to the Thessalonians (4:13–5:11) and found it necessary to correct misapprehensions in his second letter to them (2:1–17). Many Christian sects have announced the end of the world, calculating it from various biblical passages—and the earth is still revolving around the sun. Despite our absolute faith in the resurrection of the body at the end of time, we do not know what our body will look like: what, for instance, will be our age. People who die at a hundred may prefer that their resurrected bodies appear a bit younger! But how would their great-grandchildren recognize them!

No matter how strong is the biblical faith in Jesus as messiah and in Jesus' return in glory, such faith lies beyond human proof and remains "faith." We do not turn to the Old Testament to *prove exactly in detail* what happened in the past nor what would lie ahead in the messianic age. The Old Testament addresses and strengthens faith that the future happiness of God's disciples and the reward awaiting them in Jesus reach beyond all expectations, as Isaiah announced and St. Paul repeated:

> O that thou wouldst rend the heavens and come down,
> that the mountains might quake at thy presence—
> When thou didst awesome things which we looked not
> for. . . .
> From of old no one has heard
> or perceived by the ear,

No eye has seen a God besides thee,
   who works for those who wait for thee (Is 64:1–4; cf. 1
   Cor 2:8–9).

Messianic Transformation of Prophecy

Not only does the meaning of the word "messiah" have a long track record of development and modification, but the biblical application of the word to religious leaders also evolved. The Old Testament looked ahead to more than a single messiah. In fact one of the Qumran or Dead Sea scrolls, which gave the rule of life for the community, writes in the plural:

> the coming of the prophet and of the *anointed ones* (in the Hebrew, the plural of messiah) of Aaron and Israel (*Manual of Discipline* 9:11).

The *anointed one of Aaron* refers to a messiah from the priestly tribe of Aaron; the *anointed one of Israel* recalls the hopes for a new Davidic king from the tribe of Judah.

The devout Jews at Qumran, people who knew their Bible backward and forward, also expected a messianic *prophet*. In the Bible this insight shows up especially in the Elohist and Deuteronomic traditions within the five books of Moses (see chapter four). Abraham is called a prophet in Genesis 20:7. The first seventy elders are said to prophesy in Numbers 11:24–30, at which time Moses sighed and wished "that all the LORD's people were prophets, that the LORD would put his spirit upon them."

Prophecy is both a present reality in a few leaders and a future hope for all the people. When the ranks of prophets were torn by jealousy and greed, already in the lifetime of Moses (Num 12) but more scandalously in the period of the monarchy (1 Kgs 22), norms had to be provided for distinguishing true from false prophets. These are given in a more general way in Numbers 12 and more precisely in Deuteronomy 18:9–22. The latter passage was composed against false prophets who were manipulating the people through their control of secret knowledge and their supposed contact with the spirits of the other world. Deuteronomy condemns "divination, a soothsayer, or an augur, or a sorcerer, or a charmer, or a medium, or a wizard, or a necromancer" (18:10–11).

Because of the moral collapse in the ranks of the prophets, three remedies were given. One, in Deuteronomy 18, provided rules for separating true from false prophets. Another response came with Amos, Hosea and other prophets with books to their name, who became a wholly new kind of prophet. As we saw in chapter five, these at first refused the title of prophet (Am 7:14). A third response, back again in Deuteronomy 18, announced:

> The LORD your God will raise up for you a prophet like me from among you, from your brethren—him you shall heed. . . . I will put my words in his mouth, and he shall speak to them all that I command him (Dt 18:15–18).

This prophetic figure appeared, for instance, among the disciples of Isaiah (see chapter two). Anointing with oil, once restricted to kings, is bestowed symbolically upon prophecy:

> The Spirit of the LORD God is upon me,
>   because the LORD has anointed me
> to bring good tidings to the afflicted;
>   he has sent me to bind up the brokenhearted.
> [Then] they shall build up the ancient ruins,
>   they shall raise up the former devastations;
> they shall repair the ruined cities,
>   the devastations of many generations (Is 61:1–4).

Part of this passage, as we know, was quoted by Jesus and applied to himself during his inaugural sermon in the synagogue at hometown Nazareth: "Today this scripture has been fulfilled in your hearing" (Lk 4:21). Jesus did not see a single messianic moment but extended this "today" over his entire ministry.

Particularly in Old Testament times but also with Jesus the sense of a *future* prophetic leader comes clearly to the surface when there is a collapse of prophetic leadership. This is one example, among many in the Bible, of a three stage development: (a) God endows a person or an institution with promises; (b) the person or institution sometimes lives up to these hopes, but eventually collapses; and (c) in the collapse God brings to Israel's attention that the promises are still greater than they had imagined. Out of stage "c" there developed what we call "messianic promises." The transition from stage "b" to "c" is the opposite of what we would expect. If the first promises collapsed, we would anticipate God to be more practical the next time and to lower the standards. Instead, God ups the standards! Messianic fulfillment reaches beyond Bible texts and beyond our power of reasoning. It cannot be proven, only accepted on faith.

Jesus, as the *messianic prophet,* followed the style and priorities of the classical prophets, those with books to their name. These individuals did not see their mission as primarily seers and predictors of the future but as passionate champions of the rights of the poor and oppressed, as Jesus quoted these rights from the book of Isaiah at Nazareth:

> [The LORD] has sent me to proclaim release to the captives
>   and recovering of sight to the blind,
> to set at liberty those who are oppressed;
>   to proclaim the acceptable year of the LORD (Lk 4:18;
>   Is 61:1-2).

Messianic Transformation of Royalty

Messianic leadership included more than prophets. In fact, a prominent place was given to the monarchy from the fact, as we have already seen, that originally kings alone were anointed with oil. The Hebrew word "messiah" literally means "the anointed one."

Tracing the history of the messianic role of kings has its own difficulties. Kings did not belong to the original circle of leaders in the religion of Moses. A serious political crisis, one which threatened the very existence of Israel two hundred years after Moses, stampeded the people into demanding a king (1 Sam 4-5; 8).

Even though the Philistines were breathing fire down the throat of the Israelites, the people's demand for a king seemed blasphemous to the prophet-judge Samuel (1 Sam 4–5). The Israelites had to be united, they felt, as the Philistines were united. The elders, therefore, said to Samuel: "Give us a king to govern us *like the other nations*" (1 Sam 8:5; CS). Within the sadness of his heart Samuel heard God's reply: "They have not rejected you, but they have rejected me from being king over them" (1 Sam 8:7). God gave in, however, and directed Samuel to anoint Saul as king. When Saul failed, David was chosen, with still greater promises invested in him. In many different ways God writes straight with our crooked human lines. In this case a monumental advance in the religious thinking of Israel occurred through the political and military necessity of a king, forced on Israel from outside.

The next stage in the royal messianic promises came when David wanted to build a temple. That innovation was too much for God at first to tolerate, and the Lord replied through the prophet Nathan:

Would you build me a house to dwell in? I have not dwelt in a house since the day I brought up the people of Israel from Egypt to this day, but I have been moving about in a tent for my dwelling (2 Sam 7:6).

However, even this rejection is couched with a new promise:

I will raise up your offspring after you, who shall come forth from your body, and I will establish his kingdom. . . . Your house and your kingdom shall be made sure forever before me; your throne shall be established forever (2 Sam 7:12, 16).

The normal reading of this passage understands it to state that an offspring of David would be enthroned at Jerusalem forever. Yet God had another, secret, messianic message within those words.

The eternal promises were repeated at different times, gloriously in Psalms 72; 89:1–37; 132. The latter part of Psalm 89, however, groans desperately, when the incumbent king was either seriously defeated or dragged off in exile:

> How long, O LORD? Wilt thou hide thyself for ever? . . .
> Where is thy steadfast love [and] thy faithfulness thou didst swear to David? (Ps 89:46, 49).

The solution came with the prophet Isaiah. The Davidic dynasty will be cut down, with only a root in the ground. Someday, somehow God will fulfill the eternal promises and raise up a new king from this hidden and seemingly dead root:

> There shall come forth a shoot from the stump of Jesse
>   [father of David],
>   and a branch shall grow out of his roots.
> And the Spirit of the LORD shall rest upon him. . . .
> Righteousness shall be the girdle of his waist,
>   and his faithfulness the girdle of his loins.
> The wolf shall dwell with the lamb,
>   and the leopard shall lie down with the kid. . . .
> They shall not hurt or destroy
>   on all my holy mountain.
> For the earth shall be full of the knowledge of the LORD
>   as the waters cover the sea (Is 11:1–9).

This vision connects the emergence of a new Davidic king with a new paradise of eternal peace. The image of "shoot" becomes the most important title in the Old Testament for the future messianic king (Jer 23:5–6; Zech 3:8). It carries the quality of tender new life, nurtured wondrously by the Spirit of the Lord.

Two hundred years after the dynasty was toppled by the Babylonians, the author of the two books of Chronicles wrestled with the promises once made to David. The Chronicler quoted from the books of Samuel and Kings but was continuously adapting the words. When introducing the promises of 2 Samuel 7 into what is now 1 Chronicles 17, a slight but significant change was made:

I will raise up your offspring after you. . . . I confirm
him in my house and in my kingdom for ever and his
throne shall be established forever (1 Chr 7:11,14).

The phrase in 2 Samuel 7, "shall come forth from your body,"
literally in the Hebrew, "from your loins," is dropped. Biological
generation or direct succession is no longer required. God will
raise up a Davidic heir in other marvelous ways. We recall the
problem posed by Jesus' adversaries: "We know where this man
comes from; and when the messiah appears, no one will know
where he comes from" (Jn 7:27, CS).

Jesus came as king and messiah in a surprising way, born of
the virgin Mary from the inconspicuous village of Nazareth (Lk
1:26–38). Yet Jesus is still not king completely over the universe.
The prophecies of the royal messiah are still awaiting a fulfillment beyond our best understanding of the biblical texts.

Messianic Transformation of Priest and Scribe

Other forms of leadership, those of priest and scribe, were
drawn into the Old Testament portrait of the messiah. The
priesthood absorbed the privileges of royalty in the post-exilic
age. Practical necessity forced this change. The Persians had removed the governor Zerubbabel, the last survivor of the Davidic
line. Perhaps, against the Persian will, he had usurped the title of
king. The prophet Zechariah then granted the royal title of
"shoot" or "branch" to the high priest Joshua (Zech 3:8) who is
crowned as a king would be (Zech 6:9–14). Both texts are poorly
preserved and the interpretation is not at all clear. The confusion
probably reflects a confusing situation. The people, even the
leaders, were baffled at this final collapse of the Davidic line, and
were groping for a solution.

The priesthood is also drawn into Israel's messianic hopes by
prophetic visions of the new temple. Ezekiel saw a stream of fresh
water flowing from the altar of sacrifice, watering the land for a
fruitful abundance of food, even turning the Dead Sea into fresh
water (Ez 47:1–12).

Finally, the messianic image of scribe or learned person is the least clear of all, yet we see a development beyond the image of a person skilled in ancient wisdom. Proverbs 8:22–31 portrays "wisdom" with God at the dawn of creation. The rabbis transferred this image to chapter 1 of Genesis, where wisdom, now understood as the law of Moses, presided over creation—and by inference will preside over the new creation of the messianic age. This blending of wisdom, the law of Moses and the new creation is eloquently praised in the song of Sirach, chapter 24. The author draws upon the image of the four rivers of paradise, as found in Genesis, chapter 2, and sees them flowing from the Jerusalem temple, to sustain an orderly life across the earth.

In other words, in the last five hundred years before Christ, Israel was drawing upon its major institutions to sustain its hope in the messianic future. Even when these institutions were in serious decline, Israel reached into a divine mystery at their depths, to discover that God was still faithful to the original promise and would fulfill it in still more stupendous ways.

Messianic Transformation of Suffering and Brokenness

Suffering even to the point of collapse and near despair has already entered into this discussion of messianic expectations in the Old Testament. Only with the sinful degeneration and breakdown of Israel did the three main institutions of prophecy, royalty and priesthood assume their real place in Israel's messianic future. This aspect of collapse and suffering in the transformation of earlier institutions and promises will now be discussed. We turn to two different movements within prophecy: one is the suffering servant in Isaiah, chapters 40–55; the other is the cataclysmic ordeal in Daniel, chapters 7–12.

The Book of Comfort, one of the many admiring names for chapters 40–55 in the prophecy of Isaiah, opens with songs of peace echoing across the universe:

> Comfort, comfort my people,
>   says your God.
> Speak tenderly to Jerusalem,
>   and cry to her . . .

> she has received from the Lord's hand
> double for all her sins (40:1–2).

We too pulse with exalted joy as we read the following rhapsody, honoring God's care for orphaned Israel:

> Fear not, for I have redeemed you;
> I have called you by name, you are mine.
> When you pass through the waters . . .
> they shall not overwhelm you;
> when you walk through fire
> you shall not be burned. . . .
> Because you are precious in my eyes,
> and honored, and I love you. . . .
> [I say] bring my sons from afar
> and my daughters from the end of the earth (43:1–6).

In the second half of this lovely book (chapters 49–55), however, a somber sadness muffles the enthusiasm. The people could not believe that God's compassion would reach this tenderly to the ends of the earth, nor could the people accept the price of sharing the covenant and its God with other nations. Worst of all, the prophet acclaimed the Persian Cyrus as another Moses in 44:24–45:7. Such openness clashed with the narrow prejudice of the people. The prophet was spurned, publicly humiliated, cast aside. In the solitary darkness he saw himself reliving the history of his people in their dreadful suffering. He also sustained hopes beyond despair, life beyond death, absorbed from the traditions of Moses and the earlier prophets. He and his disciples wrote what are called the Songs of the Suffering Servant.

42:1–7. The silent servant achieves a victory more glorious than any conquest by the Persian emperor, Cyrus the Great. The new creation will bring light to the blind, freedom to prisoners.

49:1–7. In this autobiographical account the servant sees himself as Israel in brokenness and useless suffering, yet called to reach out and be a light to the nations.

50:4-9a. Another autobiographical account details humiliating treatment and strong defiance:

> The LORD God has given me
> a disciple's tongue,
> that I may know how to sustain with a word
> the one that is weary. . . .
> I hid not my face
> from shame and spitting.
> For the LORD God helps me . . .
> I shall not be put to shame.

52:13-53:12. In a thanksgiving hymn the sight of the silent, suffering servant brings a gasp of wonder from kings, silent contemplation from Israelites:

> Who has believed what we have heard? . . .
> He was despised and rejected. . . .
> Surely he has borne our griefs
> and carried our sorrows; . . .
> But he was wounded for our transgressions,
> he was bruised for our iniquities;
> upon him was the chastisement that makes us whole,
> and by his stripes we are healed.

61:1-4. A new prophetic call directs a disciple to surrender to the influence of the suffering servant.

These songs not only sustained faithful Israelites during darkness and frustration, but this poetry was on hand for Jesus to identify with. Jesus, however, did more than fulfill words in a book. He saw himself a member of a long tradition of faithful, persecuted servants of the Lord. Because of Jesus this hope across centuries of seemingly hopeless suffering reached fulfillment in the desolation of the cross, the silence of the tomb and the glory of the resurrection. The ideal of being a light to the nations enabled St. Paul to apply the words to his own difficult mission of preaching to the Gentiles, as in Romans 10:14-21, especially v

16, where Paul quotes Isaiah 53:1, "Lord, who has believed what he has heard from us?"

Messianism without a Messiah

The paradox of this subheading brings us before a late biblical situation where the world was so torn apart by fierce and appalling trials that it seemed that only God, no mediator or instrument, could help. The language is called apocalyptic, a Greek word for drawing aside the veil from what is most hidden. This literature teems with weird and clashing symbols; the trials and the hidden mystery explode the limits of normal words and images. Very often an angel was at hand to explain, for no human person could ever comprehend such baffling visions. One has only to read chapters 7–9 in the book of Daniel. We too repeat the words of Daniel after the first vision:

> I, Daniel, found my spirit anguished within its sheath of flesh, and I was terrified by the visions of my mind. I approached one of those present and asked him what all this meant in truth (Dan 7:15, NAB).

The vision of the four great beasts and of the ravages which they inflicted upon the holy ones of God receives its final answer:

> And the kingdom and the dominion . . .
>   shall be given to the people of the saints of the Most High;
> their kingdom shall be an everlasting kingdom,
>   and all dominions shall serve and obey them (Dan 7:27).

We are seeing a vision in which God acts immediately and definitively without the mediation of a messiah. The apocalyptic literature of Daniel is not denying the other passages which affirm a messianic mediator. It is compressing the account, due to the trauma of the moment, and focusing immediately upon God. Jesus will unpack these traditions and give them a special meaning in his mission of preaching and healing, of dying and rising, so as to be a source of instruction and life for his disciples.

Conclusion

Awaiting the messiah with the Old Testament has led us down a labyrinthine path. In its twists and turns there were familiar bursts of light. Who does not know about David and the temple? There were also long dark stretches when Israel was even more confused than we are. No one, as the prophet Jeremiah manifests in his sorrowful confessions (12:1–5; 20:7–18), thinks calmly when hounded by physical abuse and invaded by spiritual darkness.

Israel's messianic hopes developed out of its long history. Yet history was not the primary intent of the biblical writer, but rather religious instruction which emerged out of historical circumstances. Outside forces, like the Philistine threat to national existence or the Babylonian might which actually destroyed their homeland, were decisive factors forcing Israel to seek new ways of meeting their crises. These new ways were invested with hope. Yet they too failed. Out of these failures God drew a new, more profound understanding of what was wanted for the people Israel. These new hopes turned Israel's eyes to the distant future and a treasury of messianic prophecies gradually emerged. These often remained vague and uncatalogued, like our belief in the second coming of Jesus and the resurrection of our body.

Prophecies or predictions fitted in neatly with what has always been the forward momentum of the Old Testament. From the initial promises of victory in Genesis 3:15, to Moses' death overlooking the land that the next generation was to acquire, Israel's basic document of the five books of Moses made messianic prophecy very compatible.

The Old Testament remains integrally intact and yet unfinished. By itself it will instruct and comfort us, and its wide range of life meets us at every moment, innocent or embarrassing. Different New Testament writers looked to the Old Testament from different points of view, so rich was its heritage and so overwhelming the person of Jesus.

The various writers of New Testament books see the messianic role of Jesus through different sets of glasses. For Luke the glasses are ground according to the prescription of prophecy; in Acts the prescription of royalty begins to emerge. In the epistle to the Hebrews priesthood is the focal point; John's gospel frequently views Jesus as the priest and wise person presiding over the ritual of the new creation because he existed from the beginning.

The Old Testament is much more than messianic prophecy, but without messianic prophecy both Jews and Christians will find the Old Testament disappointing. How many of us, after reading the Bible, long to have lived when Jesus lived and walked by his side. For one final time we repeat: the scripture, even the New Testament, does not fix its gaze upon the past. Rather, the past with the glorious account of Jesus' life, preaching, ministry of healing, death and resurrection was put into writing that we may await Jesus in our own day. The gospels themselves are continuously turning into messianic prophecy of the second coming and our eternal, happy state with Jesus and the saints.

A few summary remarks may train our eyes to locate and appreciate the messianic movement within the Old Testament.

(1) The traditions and books in the Old Testament were composed and transmitted to new generations as a way to live holy, just lives in *their present moment*. Micah expressed it most succinctly:

What does the Lord require of you but to do justice, and to love kindness, and to walk humbly with your God (Mi 6:8).

The Old Testament does not canonize dreamers. It has little patience for those who overlook the basic expectations of justice and care toward their neighbor, prayer and worship toward God, all done with loving devotion.

(2) No single moment in the Old Testament fulfilled the hopes of God and of Israel, and so there always remained an attitude of uncompromising loyalty toward one's ideals, whatever be the circumstances. For this fundamental position of faith we turn to Isaiah:

In quietness and trust shall be your strength. . . .
The Lord waits to be gracious to you. . . .
Blessed are all those who wait for God (Is 30:15, 18).

From this position of waiting upon the Lord Israel's messianic posture was strengthened. (3) Each major institution of Israel—whether it be royalty, priesthood, prophecy or wisdom—in its glorious achievements as well as in its dismal collapses contributed to the messianic hopes of the Old Testament. Even at their best they failed to realize all that God and people of faith expected of them. In their collapse God never reneged on divine promises. Israel treasured the hopes of a new son of David, of a glorious prophetic figure, of a vindicated suffering servant, of a renewed priesthood, of a wise person enthralled at the mysteries of the cosmos. Israel, especially in its documentation among the Dead Sea Scrolls, expected several messiahs. And some of the apocalyptic literature agonized through times of colossal crisis and severe trials, and declared that God alone could overcome the chaos and re-create a new heaven and a new earth. We read from the apocalyptic finale to the book of Daniel:

There shall be a time of trouble, such as never has been since there was a nation till that time; but at that time your people shall be delivered, every one whose name shall be found written in the book. And many of those who sleep in the dust of the earth shall awake, some to everlasting life. . . . And those who are wise shall shine like the brightness of the firmament (Dan 12:1–3).

Messianic prophecy exceeds the possibilities of any institution, no matter how sacred and how endowed with divine promises. Messianic prophecy reaches beyond the potential of any individual person—unless that person be Jesus the Messiah.

Messianic promises were fulfilled in ways far beyond the dreams of everyone. A joyful, even ecstatic response of Sirach applies to messianism as it does to everything else about God in

the Bible. We conclude this book with a familiar response already
quoted in this book:

> Though we speak much we cannot reach the end,
>   and the sum of our words is: "God is all in all!" . . .
> God is greater than all divine works. . . .
> Many things greater than these lie hidden,
>   for we have seen but a little of God's works (Sir
>   43:27–32).

Index

prophetical books, 10, 15, 19,
41, 82
Protestant reformation, 18
Proverbs, 13, 40, 98
Psalms, 13, 15, 16, 36, 42,
78, 79, 81, 88, 90, 95,
96

Qumran, 12, 16, 92

Rabbi Hananiah ben Hezekiah,
17
rabbinical stories, 17
Ramah, 81
Ramses II, 42
religious assemblies, 3
Reuben, 57
Revelation, 71
ritual, 20, 30, 31
Romans, 19, 100
rubric, 43–45
Ruth, 13

Samuel:
1: 13, 14, 15, 41, 61, 81,
84, 90, 94, 95
2: 11, 13, 14, 15, 41, 61,
81, 84, 95, 96, 97
sanctuaries, 3, 39, 40, 47, 49,
55, 56, 64, 67, 68, 69,
71, 72, 74
Sanders, James, A., 4
Sarah, 46, 53, 63, 77
scribes, 74, 97, 98
Second Isaiah, 83
Septuagint, 85

Shechem, 40, 45–48, 52, 77,
80
Shiloh, 81
shrine, 58, 59
sin, 61, 62
Sinai, Mount, 14, 24, 25, 26,
28, 29, 30, 31, 32, 65,
69
Sinai (wilderness), 64, 73,
74, 77, 78
Sirach, 12, 13, 15, 16, 56, 59,
98, 104–105
Solomon, 81
Song of Songs, 13, 16
suffering servant, 98, 99, 100,
104

Tanak, 12, 13, 16
Targum, 51
temple [see Jerusalem]
theology (biblical), 17, 29,
52, 55, 75, 76, 77, 78,
79, 81, 82, 85, 86
Thessalonians:
1: 91
Timothy:
2: 9
Tobit, 15, 16, 85
Torah [see Bible]
tradition, 31, 32, 52, 57

Vatican II, 19, 20, 53, 67, 70,
75
Vulgate, 18

wilderness [see Sinai]
Wilson, Robert R., 5